The 1 Hour Trade

Make Money with One Simple Strategy, One Hour Daily

By Brian Anderson

Http://www.LanghamTrading.com

Copyright © 2014 by Brian Anderson
All rights reserved.

No part of this publication may be reproduced, stored in a retrieval system, or transmitted in any form or by any means, electronic, mechanical, photocopying, recording, scanning, or otherwise, except as permitted under Section 107 or 108 of the 1976 United States Copyright Act, without the prior written permission of the author.

Limit of Liability/Disclaimer of Warranty:
While every effort has been made in preparing this book and representing this method and its potential, the author makes no representations or warranties with respect to the accuracy or completeness of the contents of this book and specifically disclaims any implied warranties of merchantability or fitness for a particular purpose. No warranty may be created or extended by sales representatives or written sales materials. The advice and strategies contained herein may not be suitable for your situation. You should consult with a professional where appropriate. The author shall not be liable for any loss of profit or any other commercial damages, including but not limited to special, incidental, consequential, or other damages.

Free 30 Day Membership

As a way of saying *thanks* for your purchase, I'm giving you access to a 30 day Membership at www.langhamtrading.com/memberships for free.

Simply forward amazon's order confirmation email for this book to: Orders@1HourTrade.com and I will send you a promo code for the free month membership.

Table of Contents

Introduction

Chapter 1 – High Volume Runners

Chapter 2 – Basic Training

Chapter 3 – Volume and Price Action

Chapter 4 – Controlling Risk

Chapter 5 – Identifying High Volume Runners

Chapter 6 – After the Alert

Chapter 7 – Gaining Entry

Chapter 8 – Taking Profits

Chapter 9 – Chart Review

Chapter 10 – Step-By-Step Recap

Final Remarks & Contact Info

Introduction

There are very few worthwhile skills in this world, if any at all, that are easily mastered. Painstakingly difficult skills, like golf or surfing, for instance (At least for me; I'm terrible at both.), take years of regular practice just to become "good;" to become an expert takes decades.

Trading the markets is no different than these and other hard-earned skills. After years of grinding away in practice of these pursuits, the subconscious takes on an increasing role. One day you wake up, and what was once so difficult for so long now seems simple, fluid, even easy.

With almost no exceptions, there are no short cuts.

Here's the good news . . . with trading, it **is** possible to fast-track your skill. You can become a successful trader, creating income for yourself, in a very short period of time.

In order to fast-track your trading skill, you need to adopt a laser beam focus on one specific setup, follow detailed rules and parameters, and ignore all other potential trading activity until you've mastered your one setup. It doesn't have to be the one I provide in this book, but whatever setup you end up choosing, it must remain your singular focus until you have become great at it. After that, you can expand into others, one by one, mastering each before the next.

I've been trading full-time for several years. 90% of that time, I was losing money or just scraping by with marginal gains. I've made every mistake and bad decision one can make in the market. The goal of this book is to save you from as much of that as possible and get you started on a profitable setup from which you can generate an income.

During the first several years of my trading career, I studied every book I could get my hands on. I studied value investing, day trading, technical analysis, fundamental analysis, chart patterns, trader psychology, and risk management—everything and anything I thought might give me an edge.

My charts had a dozen indicators on them; I had several scanners alerting me to a number of ideal setups in real-time. I knew exactly what to look for and how to execute on many patterns and setups. I was eager and excited to make my millions in the market. Despite having all the theoretical knowledge and a firm grasp of it all, I continued to make mistake after mistake and lose money.

I suspect at least some of you have had similar experiences.

So what changed for me?

There's a saying, something to the effect of, "A dog chasing two rabbits catches neither." After reviewing my trading history, I realized I was chasing about a dozen rabbits, and I wasn't catching any of them.

I reflected on all the books I had invested in, rereading sections, reviewing notes, trying to find whatever it might be that would help me find the missing piece to success and consistent profit. During this reflection, something occurred to me.

In examining the practices of several of the most successful investors and traders, both alive and in generations past, they all have two things in common with regard to their strategies:

1. They have an extremely limited playbook, only a handful of setups they search for and commit capital to. Many have only one.

2. They have very specific rules and parameters, which their potential setup must meet.

I had overlooked this important fact and, instead, was trying to incorporate too many strategies into one plan. After this realization, I stopped trying to be a master of every trade. I stopped chasing a dozen different rabbits. I simplified. I decided, "I'm going to focus on one specific setup and become an expert at it."

My goal, formerly to "become a successful trader," became "to master three or four high reward, low risk setups, and build my success around them." With this new focused goal, I went to work. I became consistently profitable, all because I adopted a hyper-focus on only a single setup.

This book is the product of years of experience, failure, success, and education. It will teach you to create a second source of income, or significantly grow your account balance, by trading that first setup on which I built my consistency.

If you're familiar with trading, this book should be easy for you to grasp. If you're new to trading, I do my best to give you the foundational knowledge you need, but depending on how new you are, the material may be a little advanced. If you find this to be the case after you're through reading, please email me and I will answer any questions you have to get you up to speed and successful with this strategy. My contact information is at the end of the book.

The setup I've chosen for you is one I believe offers the best combination of high reward and simple implementation. It is possible to execute if you, like most people, can't spend the entire day watching the market (It only takes about an hour each morning around the market's open at 9:30am EST.) to identify the setup and execute an entry.

With that being said, you will need to have access to your account to monitor and manage your exit order throughout the day and especially before the market closes. Nearly every brokerage offers smartphone apps to manage your account, so this shouldn't be a problem.

Now please understand, **"simple" DOES NOT mean easy**. Successfully implementing this strategy and creating consistent income takes discipline and patience. These two skills can be harder to manage than every other single component of trading combined. And, unfortunately, they're impossible to gain from a book, but I try to help a bit.

I will give you a formula to succeed with step-by-step instructions, and I will outline the full range of decision making required to appropriately identify solid opportunities and capitalize on them for profits.

It is my goal to bring you to consistent income, while saving you from the high cost of "trader tuition" and the years of unprofitability most have to endure before becoming successful, if ever. As long as you bring patience and discipline to the table, this can be the start of a beautiful relationship, and you will make money.

If you can't bring the mental side, your account balance will not end well.

Let's be successful.

Chapter 1 – High Volume Runners

There are rainmakers on Wall Street—brilliant, gifted, world beating minds. They're hired by the largest hedge funds and investment banks on the planet. Some of them program trading robots, known as "black boxes" and create high frequency trading algorithms, capitalizing on arbitrage opportunities between global markets and who knows what else or what next. If you aren't one of these beautiful minds, if you didn't graduate MIT, don't worry; there is hope. You can make a living out of trading without being a rainmaker. One way is to find out where it **is** raining and hold out your bucket.

When large volume comes into a stock, there is significant price movement. It is possible to align yourself with the price movement and ride the wave of volume to big gains. I call these setups "High Volume Runners." This book will allow you to identify these stocks likely to have huge price movements, and get you into these stocks at low risk/high reward entries.

Here are some examples of these setups:

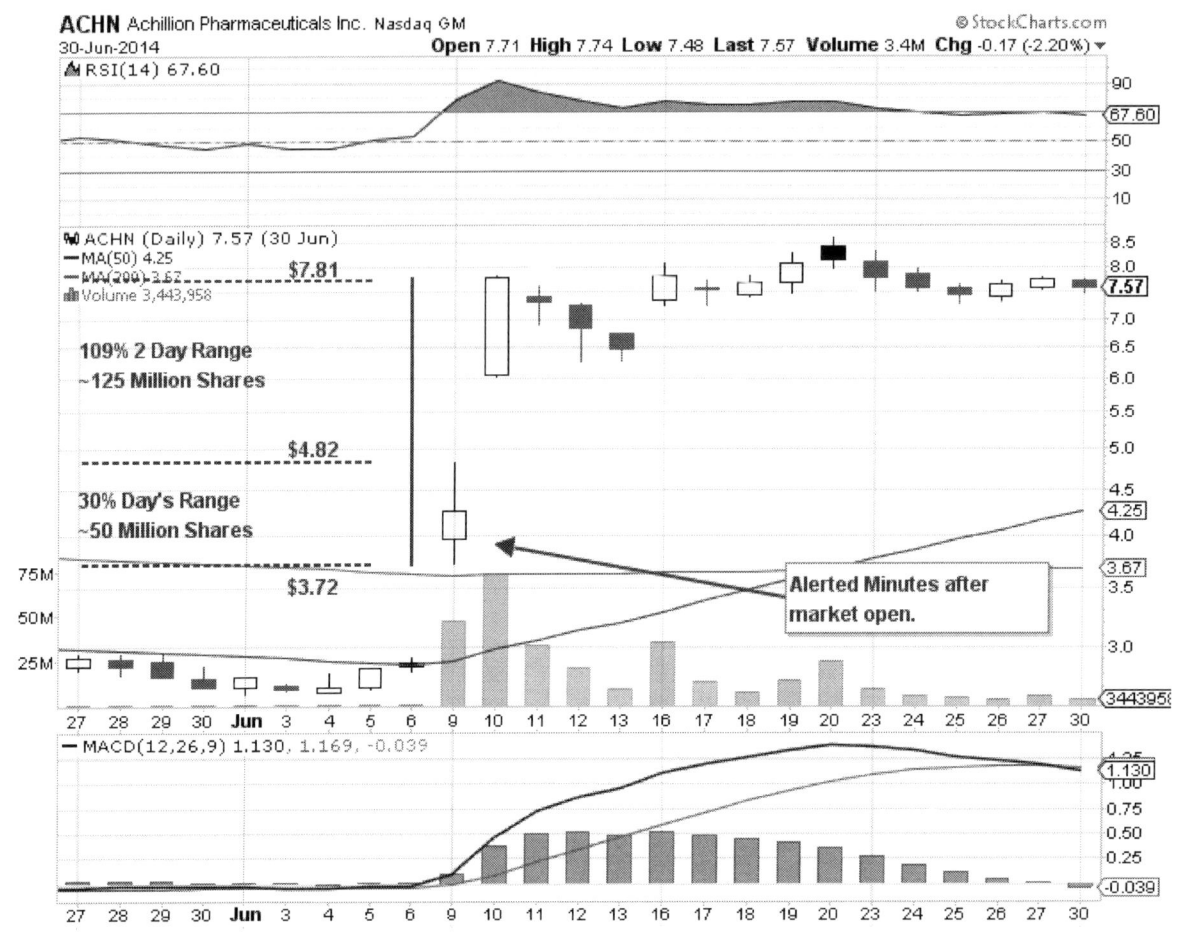

Chart 1-1

ACHN, up 109% from a low of $3.72 to $7.81 in two days. Had you captured the entire move, you would have doubled your investment.

Chart 1-2
CAMT, up 55% in a day.

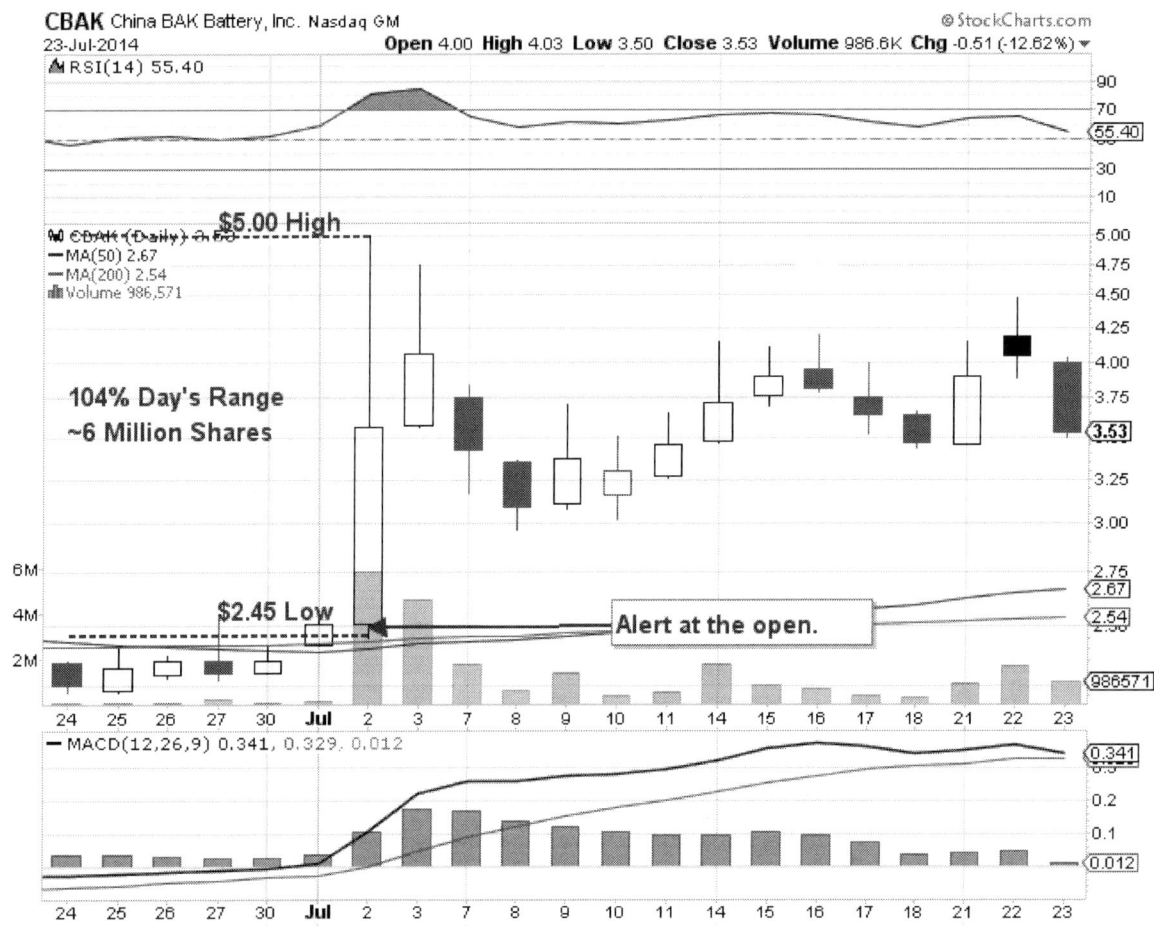

Chart 1-3
CBAK, 104% in one day.

Chart 1-4
DGLY, 188% one-day gain.

Chart 1-5
GIGA, up 195% in one day.

Chart 1-6

STEM, 21% gain in one day.

Chart 1-7
USU, gained 197% in one day, a 311% total two-day gain.

These types of movements aren't rare; all of these, and more not shown, occurred over a 60-day span or so.

The defining characteristic of this setup, other than the significant price movement, is the large increase in volume relative to the stock's average.

What happens is some kind of significant catalyst occurs, for instance a positive earnings surprise, a news story creating expectations of growth, etc. This can cause a rush of both retail and institutional buyers into the stock, which creates demand and drives the price up.

Now that you know these huge moves exist, the next several chapters will teach you the individual components you'll need to be successful at identifying them, capitalizing on them, and avoiding the ones you should stay away from.

Chapter 2 – Basic Training

This book was written assuming you have some base knowledge of trading and investing. I'll provide a quick overview in this chapter, just in case you need some brushing up on your vocabulary or basic foundational concepts. If this stuff is brand-new to you, and by the end of the book you "just don't get it," again, please email me and we'll figure out what you need.

Fundamental Analysis vs. Technical Analysis
These are two differing schools of thought when it comes to justifying an investment or trading decision.

- Fundamental analysis attempts to unravel what a company is truly worth currently and what it will likely be worth in the future, based on financial reports and underlying factors that affect the business and operations. Someone performing fundamental analysis of a stock is attempting to arrive at the value of a company in order to compare that value to the share price to determine if the current price is overinflated or undervalued.

- Technical analysis assumes that the price of a stock has little to do with its "true value" and more to do with how the buyers and sellers in the market are reacting toward its price. Someone performing technical analysis is attempting to predict where the price of a stock will be in the future, based on chart patterns and mathematical indicators.

Trading vs. Investing
Generally, "investing" describes a longer term holding period and a focus on fundamental analysis; the idea is to buy value that will appreciate over time. "Trading" describes a short-term holding period and frequent buying and selling with a focus mainly on technical analysis; the idea is to take advantage of short-term fluctuations in price.

Bulls & Bears
Those market participants who believe a stock's price will rise are referred to as "bulls" or as being bullish. Market participants who believe a stock's price will fall are referred to as "bears" or as being bearish. Buyers are bullish; sellers are bearish.

Supply & Demand
As in any free market, stock prices are determined by supply and demand. For any given stock, the current price of that stock represents the equilibrium between demand driving the price higher, and supply sinking the price lower. Those with demand for the stock are the buyers, and those with supply of the stock are the sellers.

Support & Resistance
Support is a price level that a stock has historically had difficulty falling below, due to the high demand in that particular price area. Imagine a

group of many buyers, all bidding around a certain price point; the demand pushes up against the supply at that level.

In the chart below, the support line is detailed in green:

At, and immediately below the price level represented by the green line, is where many buyers are all bidding to purchase stock. Because there are more buyers with demand for the stock than sellers with supply of the stock at that particular level, the price has difficulty sinking below that level.

Resistance, in contrast to support, is a price level that a stock has historically had difficulty rising above, due to the high volume of supply in that particular price area. In this case, imagine a group of many sellers, all selling their positions to take profits or opening short positions around a particular price level. The price cannot rise above that level because there is more supply of stock from sellers than there is demand for stock from buyers.

In the chart below, the resistance line is detailed in red:

It is important to understand that, many times, support and resistance levels behave more like nets than walls; meaning they are elastic rather than firm and static at exact price points.

Support and resistance are two of the most important ideas to understand with regard to this trading strategy because knowing these levels allows you to make better decisions about entering and exiting trades. We will discuss more on this later.

Bid & Ask and Level 2

The bid is an order from a buyer to purchase a number of shares at a specific price. The bid will detail the price offered and what quantity to be purchased. The bid volume can be thought of as demand for a stock.

The ask is the price a seller is willing to accept for her shares, also known as the offer price. The ask will detail the selling price and quantity to be sold. The ask volume can be thought of as supply of a stock.

The difference between the highest current bid, and lowest current ask, is called the "spread."

The Level 2 is a real-time view of every combination of bid price/quantity and ask price/quantity currently available for stock. Here is an example of a Level 2 screen from E*Trade:

View: Quote Montage		Find Symbol:						? Links
Symbol	Bid	Ask	$ Chg. Clo..	High	Low	Volume	Last	Size
MHP	43.39	43.40	+0.53	43.51	42.87	1,002,336	43.39	200
							43.38	100
							43.38	100
MMID	Bid	Size	MMID	Ask	Size		43.38	100
NSDQ	43.39	100	NSDQ	43.40	100		43.38	200
EDGX	43.39	100	NYS	43.40	100		43.37	100
NSDQ	43.38	312	BATS	43.40	200		43.37	100
NYS	43.38	400	NSDQ	43.41	209		43.37	100
NSDQ	43.37	762	ARCA	43.42	100		43.37	100
ARCA	43.37	400	NSDQ	43.42	1193		43.37	100
NSDQ	43.36	2851	NSDQ	43.43	630		43.37	100
BATS	43.36	100	NSDQ	43.44	554		43.37	100
TMBR	43.35	400	EDGX	43.44	200		43.36	100
NSDQ	43.35	661	NSDQ	43.45	342		43.36	100
NSDQ	43.34	939	NSDQ	43.46	100		43.37	100
NSDQ	43.33	2159	BOSX	43.49	1800		43.37	100
NSDQ	43.32	1400	PHS	43.49	1400		43.37	100
Show Order Entry		Account:			Cancel All MHP		43.37	100

For this book's purposes, all you really need to know regarding Level 2 is how to identify the volume (size) of the various bids and asks. The size of these orders gives us insight into areas of significant demand and supply that may act as support and resistance levels.

Liquidity

Liquidity is the measure of how easily a stock can be bought or sold without affecting the stock's price. The higher the trading volume, the more liquidity a stock has. Trading stocks with low liquidity is dangerous because large price changes can happen very quickly on low volume. You need to be aware of the liquidity in any stock in which you're considering opening a position. The way to judge a minimum amount of liquidity is by looking at average daily volume; stocks averaging over a million shares traded daily have enough liquidity for most trading sizes. If you're trading small positions, you can move into lower liquidity stocks safely. Just be sure there's enough minute-to-minute trading activity to allow you to exit your position size without affecting the price in any significant way.

Volatility

Volatility is a measure of the degree to which a stock's price can fluctuate. High volatility means the price can change significantly over a short period of time. In contrast, low volatility implies that a stock's price has a low range of price levels it's expected to hit for the near term future.

Order Types

Market Order – This type of order guarantees you'll be filled (Your full quantity will be purchased or sold.), but it will be filled at the available price(s) at that moment. When entering a market order, you cannot be 100% sure at what price you'll be filled until your order is complete. This type of order is useful if you need to exit or enter a trade quickly; however, it can be dangerous if the stock has low liquidity, or if the price is moving quickly. If you enter a market order when you see a stock at $X.XX, you may be filled at a much higher or lower price, depending on current volume and your position size.

Limit Order – This type of order guarantees what price you will pay but does not guarantee you'll be filled with the full quantity you're attempting to buy or sell. When entering a limit order, you dictate the price at which you're willing to buy or sell shares.

Stop Order – This is an order to buy or sell a stock when its price touches a predetermined point. Once the stock's price meets the "stop" price, a market order is triggered. These orders are effective and useful for profit protection or loss limitation, as well as breakout entries.

Stop-Limit Order – This is identical to a normal stop order, but instead of the stop triggering a market order, it triggers a limit order.

NOTE: Using stop orders will not protect against overnight price gaps.

Conditional Orders – These orders are conditional on certain events. They include contingent orders, One-Cancels-All orders, One-Triggers-All orders, and One-Triggers-OCO order. We'll go over these types of orders in Chapter 7.

Candlesticks (or Candles)

"Candles" are used in charts to detail the price action of a set period in a pictorial format. They are more useful than other forms of price action charting because they can reveal underlying sentiment (Is the current sentiment more bullish or bearish?) and potential reversals of sentiment sooner than other forms of charting. In this book when I refer to "price action," I'm referring to what the candle(s) is revealing. A candle example is shown below:

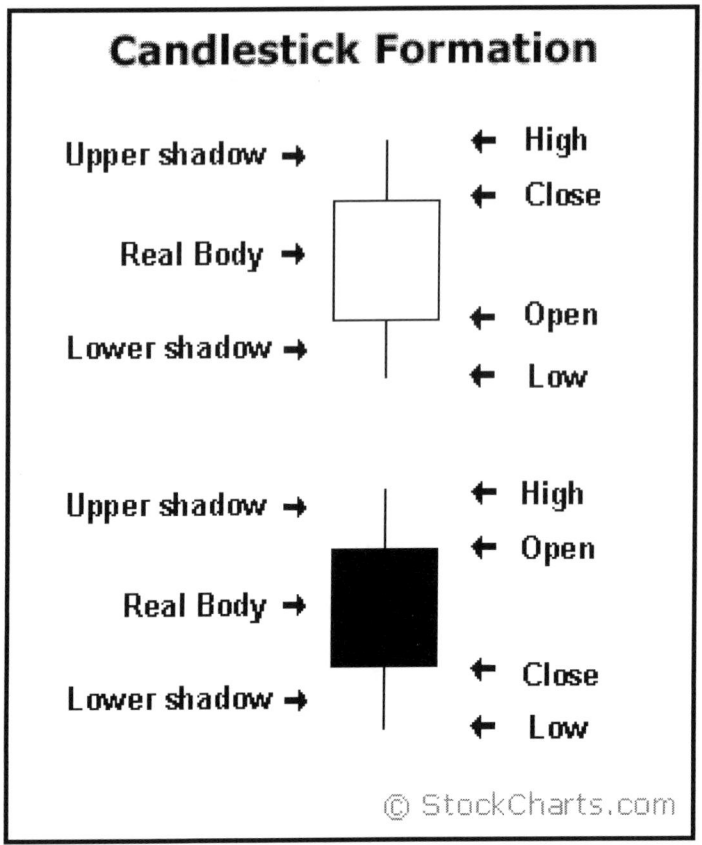

When the candle is **white (or green),** the price closed *higher* than the open for the period, so the open is at the bottom of the real body, and the close is at the top of the real body.

When the candle is **black (or red),** the price closed *lower* than the open for the period, so the open is at the top of the real body, and the close is at the bottom.

We'll go over candles in more detail in Chapter 3.

Indicators
An indicator is a mathematical calculation based on price and volume, usually represented graphically below, above, or overlaid onto a chart. There are hundreds, if not thousands, of potential indicators you can use. We use only one indicator for this setup, simple moving averages.

Simple Moving Average – SMA

An SMA is a linear representation of the average closing price over the last [x] amount of days. (For example, a 12 SMA is the simple moving average of the closing price over the last 12 days.)

Chart 2-1

We use SMAs in our setup to identify if a move is more or less likely to occur depending on where the current price is relative to various SMAs. We'll go over this in more detail later.

Gaps

- 21 -

Gaps form when the opening price creates a blank "gap" on a chart. A gap up is when the opening price is higher than the previous day's high. A gap down is when the opening price is lower than the previous day's low. Most gaps occur when there is extended-hour trading moving the pricc. They are significant when accompanied by high relative volume.

Chart 2-2

Opening Range

The opening range is the first fifteen minutes of the trading day. It is usually a good idea to steer clear of any trade commitments until you get an idea of how the price action and volume are playing out during the opening range.

HOD/LOD

High of the Day/Low of the Day

These refer to the highest and lowest prices the stock has touched so far during the trading day. Our high volume runner strategy relies on buying a break above the fifteen-minute HOD, meaning the highest price of the first fifteen minutes.

Pullback

Also referred to as a retracement, a pullback is a decline in price from a recent peak. A pullback can either be a short-term pause in upward momentum, representing a buying opportunity before the prevailing uptrend continues, or it can be the start of a full reversal in the trend, in which case potential buyers should stay away, and those holding should plan an exit.

Breakout

A breakout is a price movement through and above an established level of price resistance. Usually, a breakout is accompanied by an increase in volume and volatility. Generally, the more volume accompanying the breakout, the higher the chance it will sustain its upward momentum. A price breakout with lower volume or a lot of selling pressure in the price action is more likely to fail to continue increasing in price.

Chapter 3 – Volume and Price Action

This may well be the most important chapter in the book. If you understand the analysis of volume and its corresponding price movement, you can apply it to every potential trading setup there is. There is no indicator available that is more effective at showing you where the price of a stock is likely headed than volume when analyzed in relation to the price action associated with it (i.e. the candlestick).

Most traders today treat volume as background information—a mere afterthought to what their technical indicators are telling them. This is a mistake. If you are skilled at analyzing price action and volume, you really do not need any other indicators to be successful.

You'll need to understand candlesticks and what the different candle types signify. The price action, as detailed through candlesticks, reveals the underlying struggle between buyers and sellers and indicates where price is likely to head.

Since going into detail on the various candlestick types and patterns would take an entire book, we'll only cover the basics here. I highly recommend you pick up Steve Nison's book *The Candlestick Course* to get a more comprehensive education on the subject.

While reading this chapter, try to gain an understanding of the fundamental essence of the material. Don't get too hung up on searching charts for the exact candle types and patterns. More important than memorizing the different candle types and what they signify is an intuitive understanding of what the individual candle's various components (upper and lower wicks, real body, red or green) are detailing about the underlying struggle between buyers and sellers.

Candlesticks

Again, here is the anatomy of a candlestick:

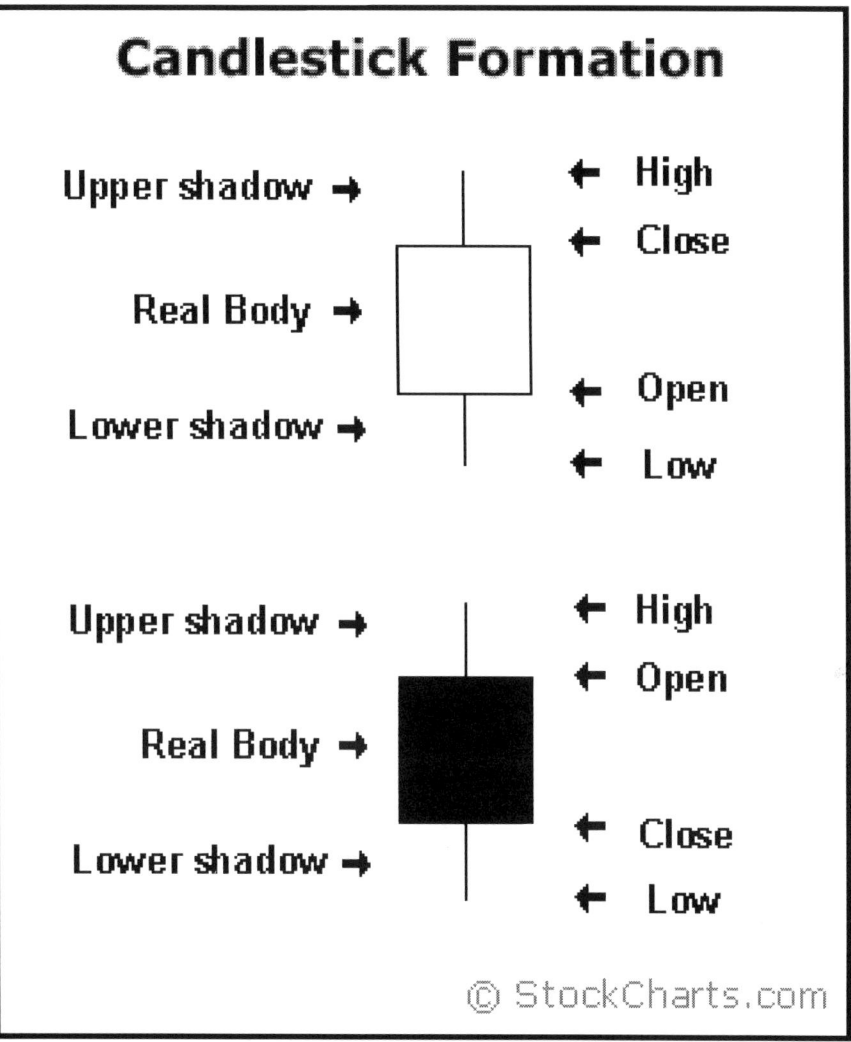

White or green candles represent a price move higher than the open of the period, while black or red candles represent a price move lower than the open of the period.

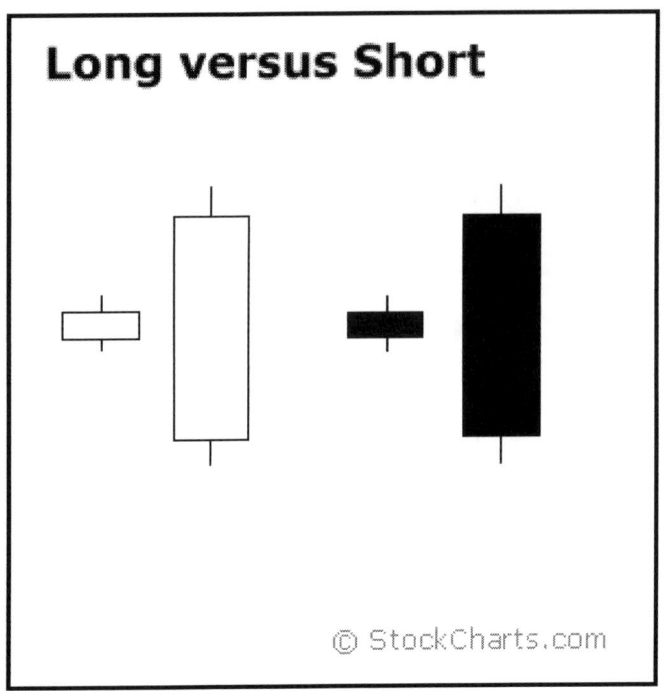

Short candles detail a tightly bound price range between the opening price and closing price of the period, while long candles detail a significant price movement/range between the opening price and closing price of the period.

Long candles (big price movement) associated with large relative volume (big supply/demand) are what you'd expect; this means either the bulls (buyers) or bears (sellers) are firmly in control of the movement. A high volume of supply from bears would be expected to create a large drop in price. A high volume of demand from bulls would be expected to create a large rise in price.

In contrast, **short candles (little price movement) are what you'd expect with low relative volume (little supply/demand)**.

What to Watch For

If you see a short candle (little price movement) with high relative volume (big supply/demand), this should cause you concern.

A short candle (little price movement) with large volume (big supply/demand) could mean the current trend is weakening, that the side that was previously in control is running into resistance or support. The large volume of buying (demand) or selling (supply) isn't moving the price because the opposite side is coming in strong at that price level and preventing the significant price movement expected.

Conversely, if you see a long candle with low volume, this could signal the move is running out of steam and reaching the final run before a reversal comes in.

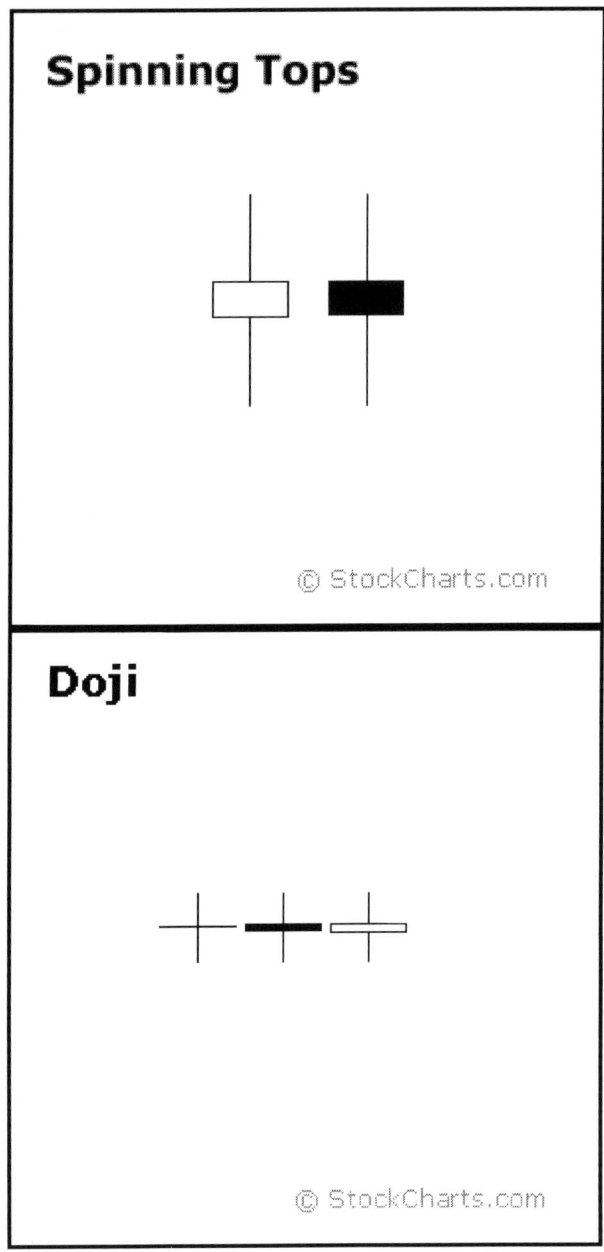

Spinning tops are candles that detail large price movement between the high and the low; however, the open and close are closely bound or equal. Doji are candles that detail a tight range between the high and the low, as well as the open and close. What these candles are signifying is that there's a considerable struggle going on between buyers and sellers, with neither controlling the price action.

What to Watch For: Watch for these to signal potential reversals or retracements in either an uptrend or downtrend; it details a struggle over control of the price movement between bulls and bears. If you see this candle, put your guard up and look for the next candle to confirm the signal. For example, in an uptrend, if the next candle's price moves on to break above the recent high, then the bulls regained control, and the trend is likely to continue; a move below the recent low is a good indication the bears took over, and the trend will reverse down until another signal appears and/or the price finds a support level.

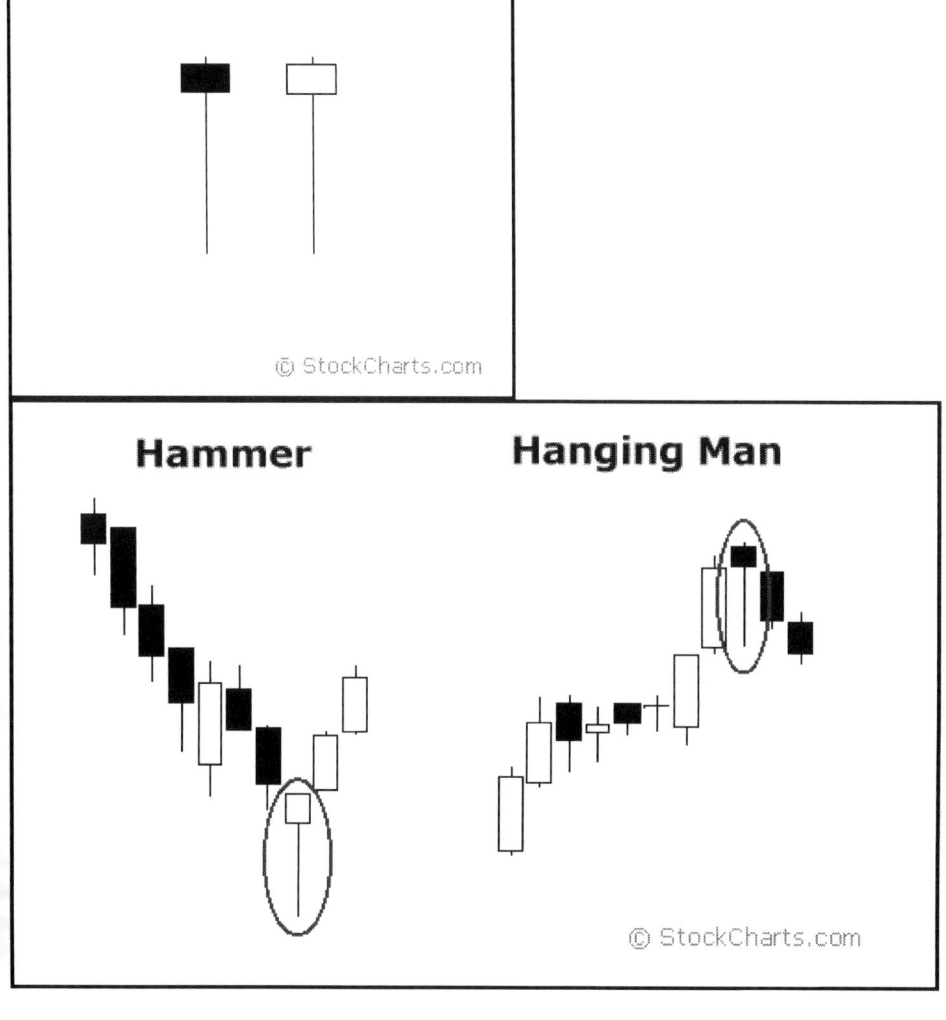

A Hammer or Hanging Man is a candle with a long lower wick, small real body, and little or no upper wick. These signal potential reversals. As you can see from the graphic, the candle is called a hammer when appearing in a downtrend, and a hanging man when appearing in an uptrend.

What to Watch For: Think about why these candles signify reversals; what is happening according to the candle? In a downtrend, the bears control the price action, forcing it down until the bulls say "this price has gotten too low" and take over, forcing the price to recover most of the losses and close near the top, hence the long lower wick and small real body at the top.

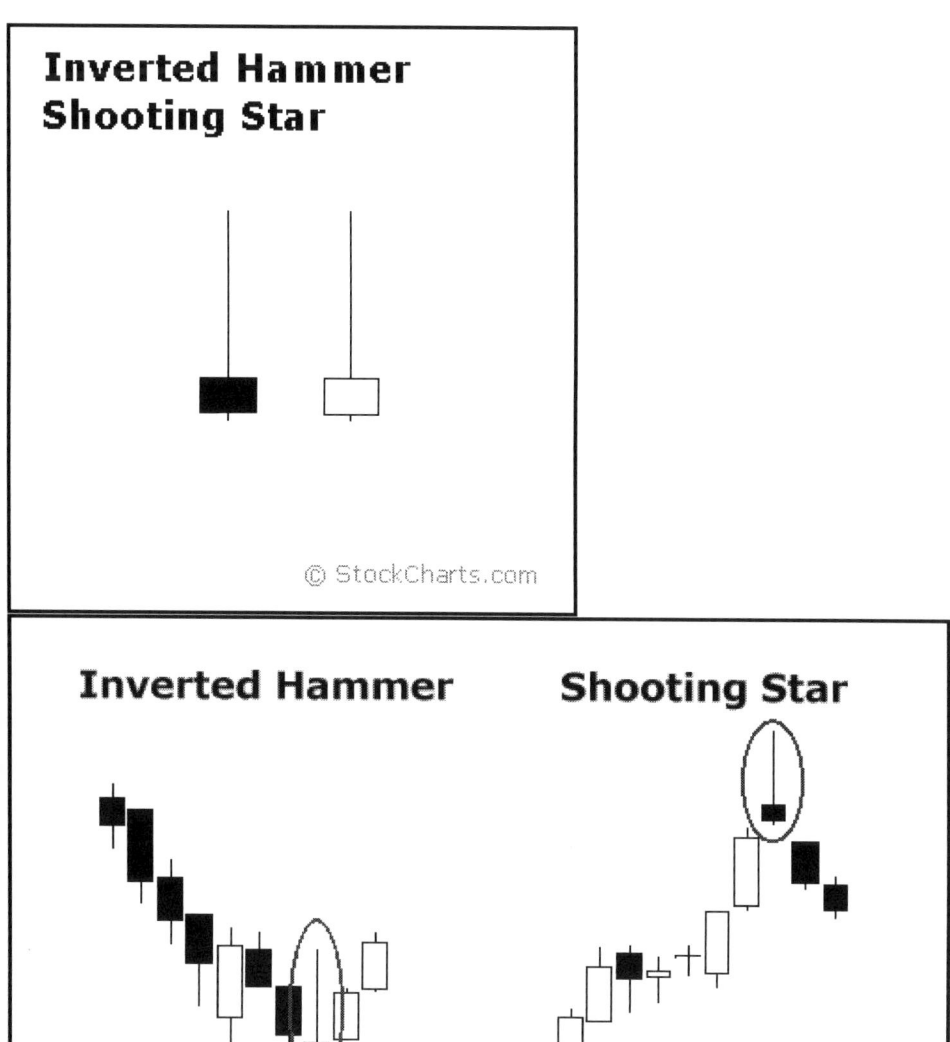

An Inverted Hammer, or Shooting Star, is similar to the Hammer and Hanging Man, the difference being they have a long upper wick instead of a long lower wick. These signal the same potential trend reversals.

What to Watch For: Again, try to understand what is fundamentally happening under the surface. During a downtrend when an inverted hammer appears, the long upper wick represents buyer strength coming into play, driving the price up, though giving it away to the sellers to close at the bottom of the price range. It signals a potential reversal because the buyers are no longer as weak as they have been during the previous downtrend. The opposite is true of a Shooting Star, which appears during an uptrend.

This should give you enough of a foundation on candles to get you going with the high volume runner setup. You'll get better at identifying the underlying action of price movement as you put your analysis into practice.

And remember, it's more important to understand the essence of what the candles are indicating than to know every different candle type or multi-candle pattern. As long as you can look at the candles and understand what the components are telling you, you'll be successful.

Before we move on, and this is important, understand that no single candle should be used to make any decision about entering or exiting a trade—ever. You must have patience. You need to consider the whole picture by identifying support and resistance, analyzing the price action and associated volume, and looking at multiple time frames to confirm what is happening and what is likely to happen.

Now on to volume . . .

Volume – The Only Thing That Matters
I have a trader colleague who is very big on "trading the news." He has CNBC constantly running in the background of his office; he has a dozen different internet windows open to all the major financial news outlets. He believes he can get information through news, which can effectively be used as an edge to trade profitably.

I asked him about it, and he said, "News moves prices." I replied, "No it doesn't; buyers and sellers move prices." He rolled his eyes, saying, "You know what I mean; the news causes buyers and sellers to move prices." That argument went on, and in fact still does. In contrast to my colleague's methods, I have completely abandoned all news sources for trading ideas.

I'll admit, on a certain level, he's correct; a piece of news can be used effectively for a profitable trade, as the news causes a large amount of buyers or sellers to come in and move the price. The momentum that they create can be traded for profit. However, I argue that the same trade could be had without any knowledge of the underlying news, and that coming upon trades this way—without knowing the news—is much more likely to result in success. I'll explain . . .

When relying on news for trading ideas, you are making questionable assumptions:

1. You assume the piece of news you found is significant enough to move the price at all.

2. You assume you've identified the news before the coming price movement, that the market hasn't already priced the news into the stock.

3. You assume you're able to accurately analyze which direction that particular news is going to drive the price.

If the idea is to find news likely to cause enough volume to effect significant price movements, why not just look for the volume, and let that volume and price action dictate what's likely to happen and, in fact, what *is* actually happening, so you can plan your entry appropriately?

News **can** cause large volume spikes, but why waste time and resources and trust your uncertain conclusions, trying to position your entry before a price movement that may or may not come?

Who cares what the news is, if you can find the volume and capitalize on the price movement without it?

Volume never lies. Volume is much more easily analyzed than news, and scanning for large volume is infinitely less time consuming than scouring the internet for news, which may or may not result in a good trade setup.

Volume reveals the validity of price movement. It is the great equalizer between insiders and retail investors. If you know how to find volume and how to analyze volume, almost nothing can be hidden from you—not institutional buying, not underlying bullish or bearish market sentiment, not the likely direction of future price movement.

At a minimum, you need to understand this fundamental idea:
    A. Price movements with high relative* volume should be assumed valid, and price movements with low relative volume should not override what the higher volume price movement is telling you (*"relative" to the average volume for that particular stock).

Here's a five-minute chart detailing how volume and associated price action detail the likely future movement of price. The thought progression is numbered.

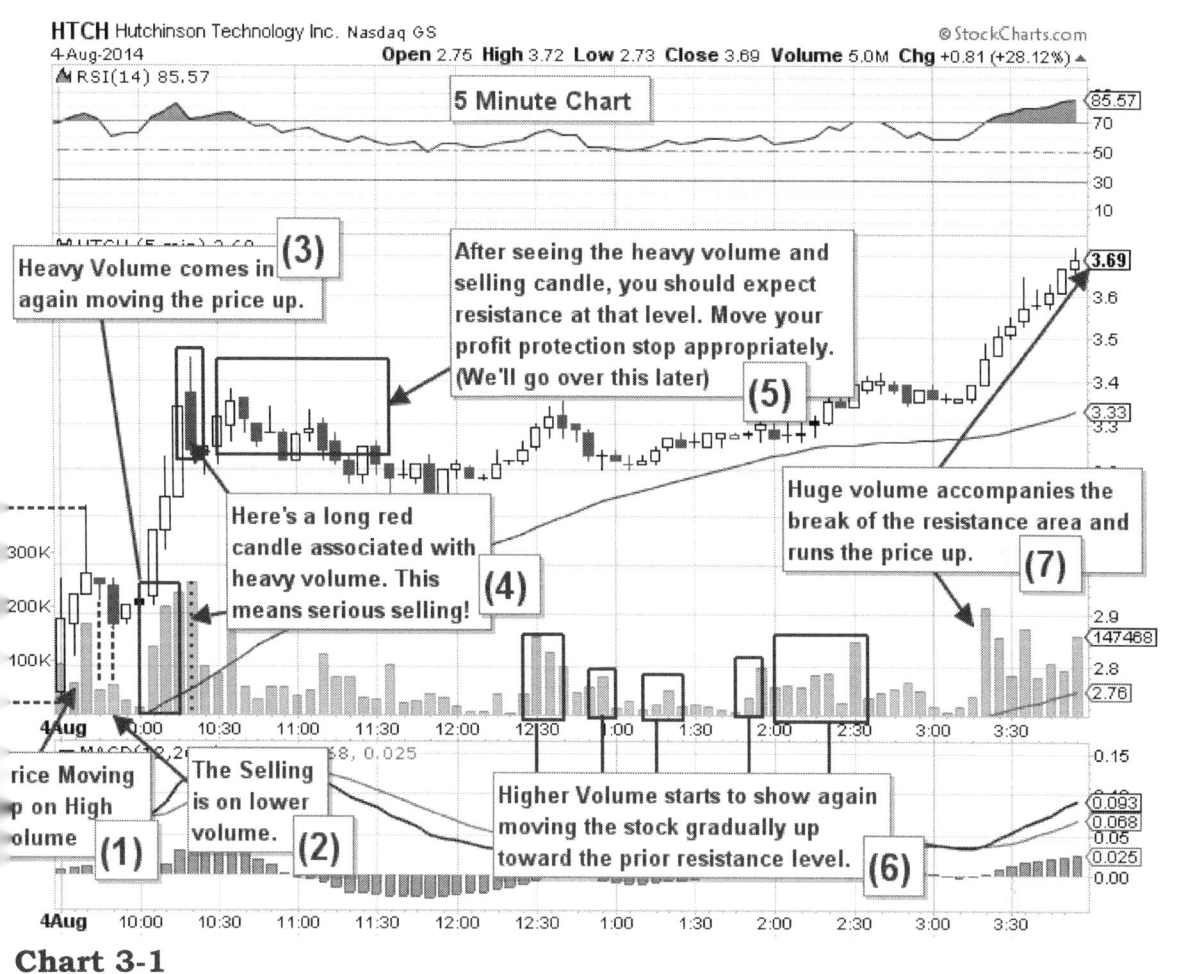

Chart 3-1

Although the third candle appears to have a lot of selling pressure with the long upper wick, this is a five-minute chart; when seen through a 1-minute chart, the upward price movement is associated with high volume, and the selling that caused the long upper wick on the five-minute candle is on very low volume when viewed through 1-minute increments. This is why it is important to analyze volume and price action using different time frames.

There are no hard ratios or indicators telling you when a price move is valid. You can't make a decision based on X number of shares traded or the fact that candle was X/Y ratio of average price, etc.

- 35 -

The analysis of price action and accompanying volume is something that you'll need to practice to get a feel for, but once it "clicks" for you, it will serve you better than any other indicator out there and will help you execute much more successful and profitable entries and exits.

Chapter 4 – Controlling Risk

Ideally your pre-trade review, which we'll get to in Chapter 6, should keep you from entering trades that don't have a high probability of success. Even with that being the case, we always run the chance that we may have more losing trades than winning trades.

That is ok.

While I won't get into the mathematics which proves it, trust me when I tell you that a high winning percentage is not important; what IS important is ensuring the AMOUNT of your gains is more than the AMOUNT of your losses.

This setup, when followed properly, will provide big gains for you. As long as you follow the rules and exit losers for small losses and let the winners run, you'll be profitable.

That is assuming you manage your money and trade size appropriately, as well as maintain discipline.

Money Management
First things first; you need to know how much money you are going to risk per trade. Never risk more than 1% to 3% of your total account balance on any one trade. To calculate your per trade maximum loss, simply multiply your account balance by your chosen risk figure (1-3%).

For example, if your risk tolerance is 2% per trade and you have an account balance of $8,000, your maximum allowable loss on any one trade is $160 (.02 x 8000). It should include entry and exit commissions, so conservatively we'll say the maximum loss per trade is $140 (This is the amount you can lose if your stop is hit, not the amount of capital you commit to a trade.).

The reason I like this method is because as your account balance grows, it allows your trading size to grow; however, if your account balance is decreasing, it lowers the amount of money you can lose on any one trade.

The next step is calculating the maximum number of shares you'll be allowed to purchase while honoring your maximum allowable loss. This number will differ from trade to trade depending on the price of your stop-loss exit and your entry price.

In the high volume runner setup, we will usually know our stop-loss before our actual entry price.

To figure out how many total shares you can purchase in a trade (i.e. your maximum position size), divide your maximum allowed loss by the price difference between the stop-loss price and estimated average holding price.

For example, assume you're considering a setup where the stop-loss exit is $3.54, and the current price is $3.62. Taking the $140 maximum allowed loss we calculated above, divide that by $0.08 ($3.62 - $3.54 = $0.08), and you get 1,750 as your maximum position size (140/.08 = 1750).

I've provided an Excel spreadsheet that will quickly calculate the position sizing figures for you here: www.langhamtrading.com/tradesize. However, you need to be able to quickly calculate this stuff in your head, because these high volume runner setups move quickly. Practice your mental math muscles as much as possible.

Account Size

Here's a story that is well worth noting: On July 16th (2014), Nasdaq halted trading in NewLead Holdings (NEWL) **in the middle of trading hours** at a price of $4.38, after hitting a high of $5.03 that day. NEWL went on to get delisted from Nasdaq.

On July 22nd, it reopened at $2.55 and plummeted from there. This type of trading halt and subsequent delisting rarely happens, but be aware that it does. And life isn't fair; it could happen to you.

By the way, there were over 30 MILLION shares traded in NEWL the day it was halted. A lot of people lost a lot of money that day.

I'm sure you've heard before, "Don't trade with money you can't afford to lose." This is a little unrealistic, in my opinion, and seems more like a disclaimer than actual advice. Here's some honest advice: be conservative, never risk more than 1-3% of your capital on any one trade, be very careful any time you have more than 25% of your total capital at play in any one trade, and just be aware of the risk involved in trading, even intra-day trading.

Be smart.

If your account balance is under $25,000 (and you have a margin account), you'll be subject to "pattern day trading" restrictions, which means you can't make over three trades in a rolling five-day period. It's a ridiculous law, but you are at its mercy nonetheless. Make sure you're aware of your online brokerage's particular treatment and interpretation of pattern day trading (Some brokerages count multiple orders of a single stock as one trade, while others count each separate purchase as a new trade).

The pattern day trading restrictions do not apply to cash accounts (non-margin) under $25,000, but "Free Riding" restrictions do. Free Riding is another idiotic SEC restriction, but, alas, you are subject to it nonetheless.

For reasons I can't fathom in this day and age, stock transactions with your online broker take three days to settle. You cannot use the proceeds from a sale of stock to purchase another stock until the proceeds from the sale have "settled." This means if you're in a trade utilizing your full account balance, and you exit, you won't have access to that balance to place another trade for three days.

Bottom line, if you're working with a non-margin account under $25,000, you must be selective with your trades; only enter ideal setups (We'll get to how to identify ideal setups shortly).

Psychology
Equally important to managing your risk is your mental discipline.

When I was consistently losing money or just scraping by with marginal gains, I would often enter market orders when I found a stock I wanted to enter. I was always fearful that I had found a huge trade but it was taking off that moment, seconds after I had located it; if I didn't get in now, I would miss it.

After I shifted my mindset to the new thinking of "master only a few setups," I stopped chasing entries. I rarely placed market orders any longer, unless it was acceptable per the parameters of the setup (We never use market orders in this setup). In most of my setups now, I put a tight range of bids where I believe strong support to be, so I have a low risk stop under my entry level. Many times I miss trades, but that is ok; there are others soon to come.

That newly found patience made a huge difference in my profitability. Rather than hitting the market to enter a trade, I patiently sat with bids at a level where fear would drive the emotional traders out, and they'd sell into support. If you see an area of support but you think the trade has moved above it, never to return, think again. It may take a few days or even weeks, but it will come down again to allow a low risk, high reward entry. And If it doesn't, you've lost nothing.

The creative part of your mind is your enemy. The emotions you'll feel, the hopes and wishes you have for the trade, your opinion about where the price is going, the fear that you're going to miss out on a profit if you don't get into the trade at this very moment—all these thoughts are working against you. You need to turn off everything but the analytical, rational part of your mind. This is easier said than done, but there are tools that can help.

One is your stop-loss order.

Do not use a mental stop. As soon as you execute an entry order, execute the stop-loss order to sell. Then move it higher to the break-even point as soon as the price action allows (more detail on this later). In this setup, you'll be able to enter a conditional order, which will execute your stop order automatically as soon as your purchase order is filled.

You need to develop a mantra:

> "There will always be another trade."

Learn it, know it, live it.

Above all else, be patient. Weeks or more may go by without a valid, optimal green flagged setup appearing. Hold steady and trust that one is coming; these setups will continue to show themselves. You cannot force a good high volume runner setup.

Patience alone can actually be enough of an edge in the market to be successful, as long as it's patience for a good entry. Patience has no place in a losing position; exit your stop-loss immediately, and let your winners run.

It is ok to miss a trade. The worst thing you can do is hit a market order because you think the stock is running, and you believe you've missed the entry. The chances of your market order nailing the ideal price at the exact moment of your execution are next to nil.

Every dollar you lose trying to force a trade or chase an entry is a dollar that isn't there for you when a 50%, 100%, 200%+ runner shows up. Only enter a trade according to the low risk parameters of this setup, which we'll get to.

Never chase an entry. There will always be another trade. And one final time for good measure . . .

NEVER CHASE AN ENTRY. THERE WILL ALWAYS BE ANOTHER TRADE.

Chapter 5 – Identifying High Volume Runners

In order to be alerted in real-time to the high volume runner setup, you need to choose an online brokerage that has real-time scanning and alert functionality. I use E*Trade Pro; it is free if you place at least 30 trades per quarter. Otherwise, it is $99 per month. The scanning functionality is well worth its cost if your account balance is at least $2500. Below that and the cost becomes a little prohibitive compared to the returns you need to cover the $99.

Feel free to use other online brokerages, but make sure they offer real-time scanning and can accommodate the parameters detailed in this chapter.

We're going to setup two scans working in tandem to locate our high volume runner setups.

The first scan (in E*Trade Pro, under the Strategy Scanner tool and "Create Your Own Strategy")
is going to have the following parameters:

Alert Type: "Unusual Number of Prints" = [30] as the Ratio.
    This means you're scanning for stocks with volume that is at least 30 times higher than average for the time of day.

Filters:
1) Minimum Price = $1.00, Maximum Price = $10

- We can't spread our search too broad, or we'll be inundated with alerts and won't be able to analyze them all. I choose this low price range because they are more likely to have serious price movements than higher priced stocks. You may even consider going with $0.50 to $5, or $1 to $8—whatever you're comfortable with.

2) Volume Today = $30,000$ Minimum
   - In the past, I've had this number set higher, but a few times it caused me to miss the early formation of a high volume runner. The trade off in lowering it is you get alerted earlier. However, it will, at times, give you stocks that aren't liquid. A quick glance at the chart will reveal if this is the case, if liquidity isn't high pass on the trade.

3) "Change from the Close" = 4% Minimum Value
   - Stocks that are trading at least 4% above the previous day's close.

4) Time of Day = Set the "maximum" to 20 minutes after the open.
   - If you have the time to watch the market during the day, you can expand this variable so you receive alerts later in the day. However, the longer the time has passed from the open, the more likely the alerts will be for very illiquid stocks.

Symbol List:
Only check "NYSE," "AMEX," and "NASDAQ." Otherwise, you'll be getting too many stocks that aren't liquid enough and aren't traded on the major exchanges.

We also use a second scanner that searches for big gainers; it puts a bit of redundancy in place so we're less likely to miss big moves. There have been times when a stock should have been alerted on the main scan but wasn't. After that happened a few times, I just decided to have this secondary scan to double up the search efforts.

Second Scanner Settings:
Alert Type: "% Up for the Day" = [6] as the Minimum % Up

Obviously, this means you're scanning for stocks at least 6% up from their open for the day.

Filters:

1) Minimum Price = $1.00, Maximum Price = $10
   - This should match whatever you set your primary scan price range to.
2) Volume Today = 30,000 Minimum
3) Time of Day = Maximum is 20 minutes after the open.

Symbol List:
"NYSE," "AMEX," and "NASDAQ"

Again, if you don't want to go with E*Trade, make sure the online brokerage you do go with can accommodate these parameters before you sign up with them.

Another option is to sign up for a subscription at www.langhamtrading.com.

If you email the order confirmation for this book to Orders@1HourTrade.com, you'll receive a Month of Free Access, even if you ordered the book for free.

We'll perform the pre-trade analysis/review work for you, and only alert you to the trades that pass the review process complete with entry and exit targets/parameters. We trade additional proven strategies there as well.

Once an alert hits, we need to evaluate its potential for a large movement in price.

The way we do that is through analysis of the chart on three separate time frames, while applying a "Red Flag" checklist and a "Green Flag" checklist.

We'll get into those details now . . .

Chapter 6 – After the Alert
(The First Fifteen Minutes of the One-Hour Trade)

So you've got the scanner setup, and you start getting alerted to potential setups. Here's what you do now.

Step One – Triple Time Frame View
Pull up the stock on three charts:
1. Weekly 2-Year Chart
2. Daily 1-Year Chart
3. 5-Minute Chart

Step Two – Red Flag/Green Flag Review
This review is done both on the weekly and the daily. The goal is to analyze the charts to determine whether the potential runner is likely to run or should be disregarded.

Red Flag Review:
1. Resistance
   - If there is a significant resistance level immediately overhead, be wary. It might be best to disregard the trade. If resistance is high enough above the current price to allow for a significant gain, then you're ok.

2. Large abrupt selloffs in the nearby past
   - Former buyers will hold through these crashes, hoping for a chance to sell at a small loss or break even.

3. Large Gaps Up
   - The larger the gap, the more attractive it is for traders on the short side to "fade" the move, looking for the gap to fill at least a portion of the area toward the pre-gap pricing. With a large gap up, you'll be battling these sellers in many cases.

4. **30, 50, or 200-Day SMA Lines Above?**
   - If there are significant moving average lines above the current price, it could cause resistance.

If any of these red flags are present, you should be conservative. If multiple flags are present in combination with one another, just pass on the trade.

Chart 6-1 shows an alert with multiple red flags:

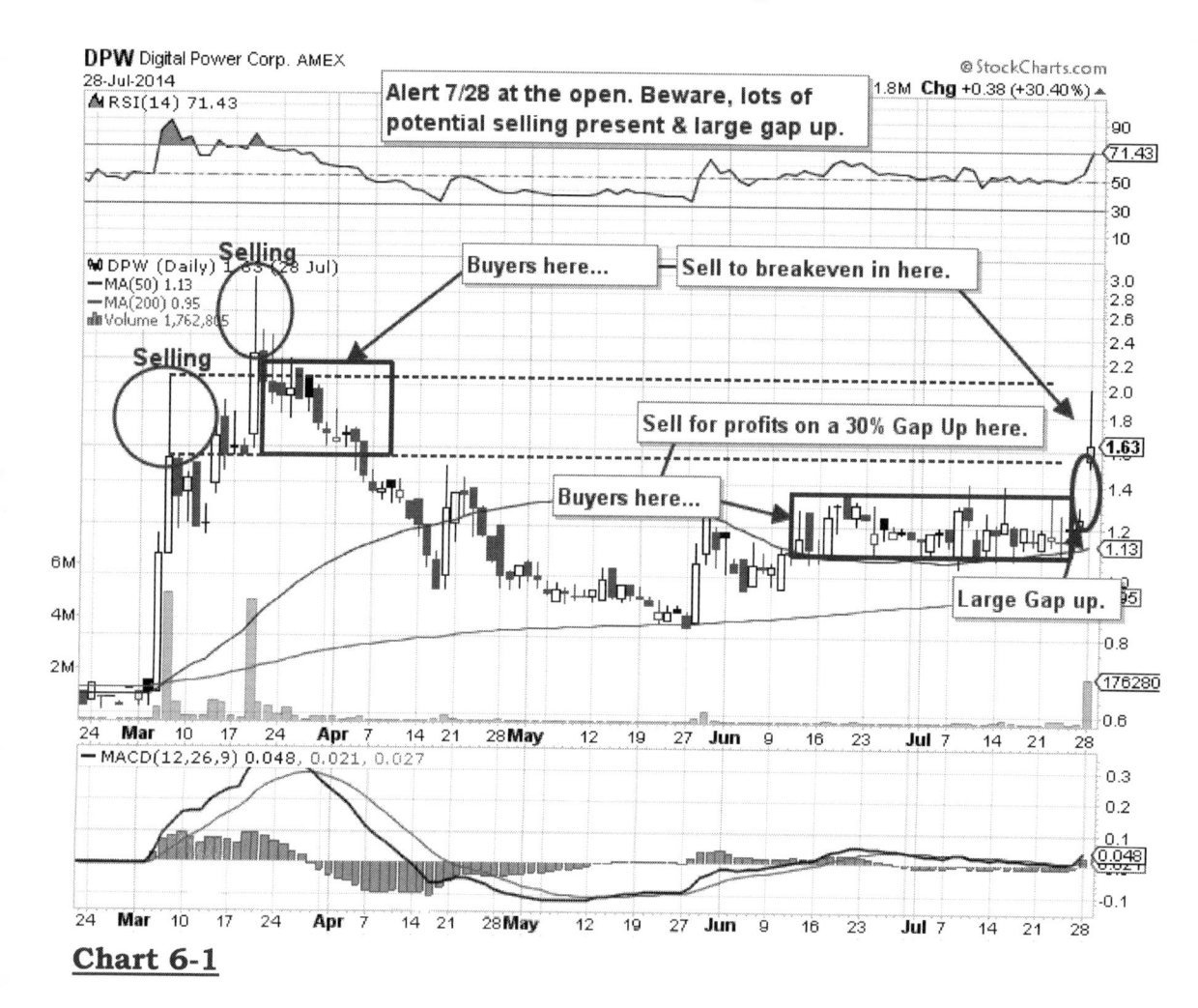

Chart 6-1

- 48 -

There are lots of red flags present here. There is a large gap up, approximately 30%, so there are a lot of profit takers scrambling to sell, as well as short sellers trying to fade that large gap. You also have former buyers from the prior months that held through their major account balance declines getting out for a small loss or a chance to break even.

Green Flag Review

These are the ideal conditions we're looking for in a potential runner:

1. Support
   - Is there significant longer-term support immediately under the current price level?

2. Is price action the last 3-12+ months in a tight range with no significant volume?
   - The longer the period of a tight price range and low volume, the better chances the stock will run big.

3. Did the price just set a new long-term high, or will it if it breaks out of this morning's opening fifteen-minute range?
   - New longer-term highs tend to have lower selling pressure; selling won't be a significant factor until profit taking starts.

4. Is the stock breaking above its 200-day and/or 50-day moving average?
   - A break of these levels is a favorite long entry for many traders; more buyers coming in will continue to drive prices higher.

The more of these green flags confirmed, the better the potential for serious upward price movement.

Here's an example of a chart with ideal conditions; it's the same stock, DPW, a few months prior to the red flag alert detailed prior:

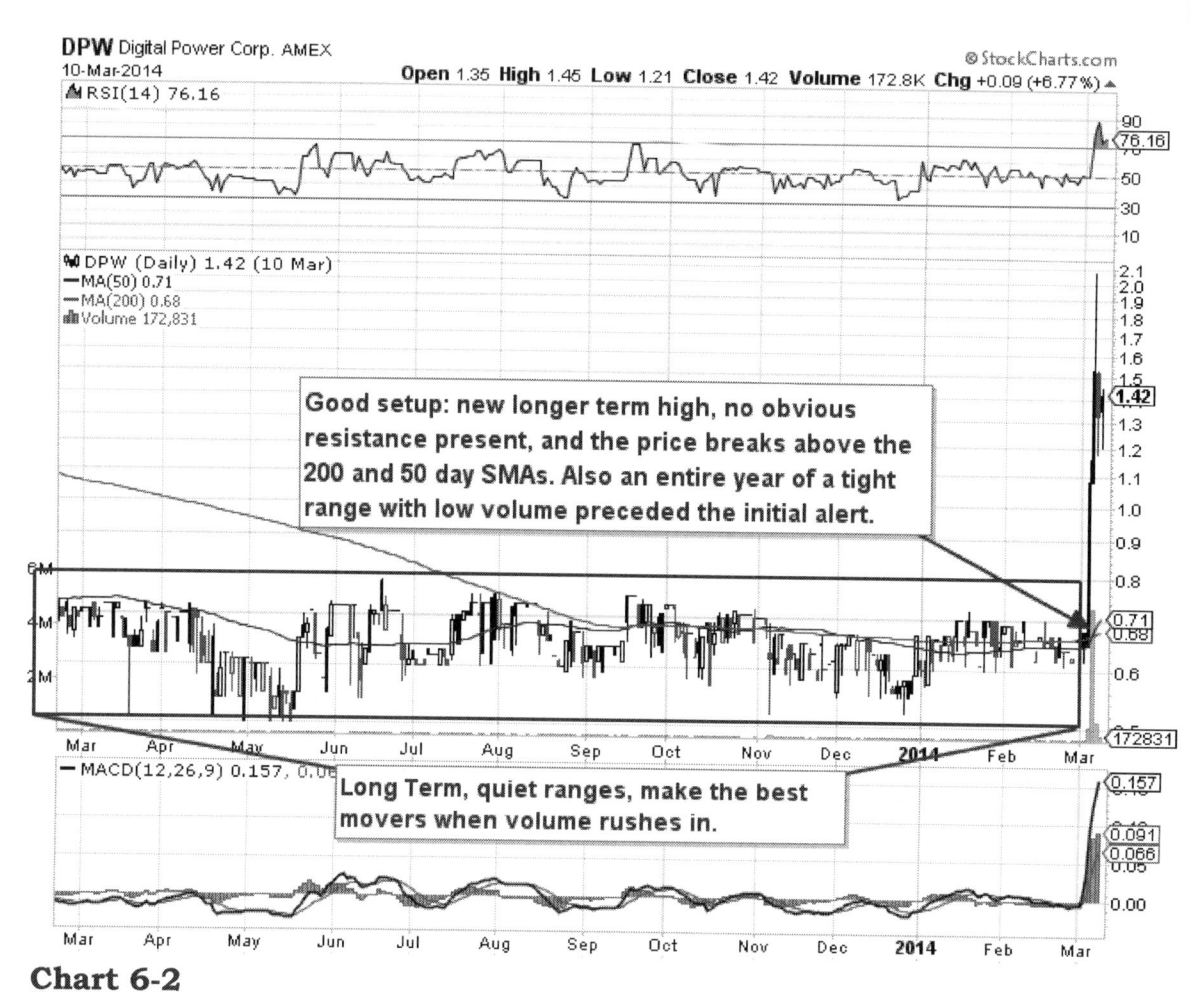

Chart 6-2

As you see here, the alert in early March is a solid setup. There was a long-term, tight range with very low volume, there is no significant resistance to be found, no recent selloffs, it is breaking into a new long term high, as well as breaking above both the 200-day and 50-day moving averages. It goes on to a nearly 100% range and around five million shares traded that day.

- 50 -

Chapter 7 – Gaining Entry

A quick note: this chapter was originally going to contain a pullback/low of the day entry option in addition to the standard entry for this setup. I've decided to omit the pullback entry because while it can put you into much more profitable entries, there is a lot involved in deciding when it should be used; and it shouldn't be used very often. At the end of the day, I thought it would serve you better to leave it out.

I will be putting out a separate blueprint for the pullback/low entry in the near future, which will apply to both the high volume runner setup as well as setups with longer term holds. If you're interested in this, drop me an email at brian@1hourtrade.com, and I'll put you on the distribution list.

On with Chapter 7 . . .

The entry we'll use for our high volume runner setup is a breakout entry. It has a low risk to reward for this setup and will keep you out of trades that do not have the momentum to continue a big run past the opening range high.

It is optimal for those of you needing to be selective with your trading activity to avoid pattern day trading or "free riding" restrictions. In addition, it allows for plenty of time to analyze your stop level, entry price, and trade size.

The entry is triggered when the price of the potential high volume runner breaks above the highest price of the first fifteen minutes.

The best way to enter the order is with a conditional One-Triggers-All order. With a One-Triggers-All order, you place your buy order and stop-loss order at the same time; if the buy order is executed, the stop-loss order triggers. For the buy order we use a stop-limit; for the stop-loss sell order, we use a stop-on-quote.

Stop-Limit Order
When creating the One-Triggers-All Order, the stop price is set at $0.01 above the high of the first fifteen minutes.

The limit price for your purchase is set according to your preference and in consideration of your situation; here are your options.

    A) Set the limit price for purchase a few cents higher than the stop price. Usually, the price will dip back to the breakout point if not below it. However, some big runners will break out and never touch the breakout level again. So setting the price a few cents higher than the stop will get you into most setups successfully.

    B) Set the limit price at or a few cents lower than the stop price. Again, many setups will dip back below the breakout price before heading higher; this will get you into the setup at a lower price and expose you to a lower per share price risk. However, you could miss a setup that moves fast.

    C) Identify a support level on the 1-minute chart, and use that level as your limit purchase price.

Stop-Loss Order

The sell order portion of the conditional order is a "stop-on-quote order," and you have to decide where to put the stop. You have a couple of options:

A) You can set the stop-loss price $0.01 below the former high. I would urge against this. Many times a runner will dip back below its former opening range high before finding buying momentum again and running higher. If you set your stop this close to your entry, you can get stopped out too easily and miss a good run.

B) You can set the stop-loss at a point below a "whole number" where usually you'll find buying support. This isn't a bad option when the round number is below the entry level enough to avoid being stopped out on normal levels of price volatility.

C) You can set the stop-loss below the pullback low of the opening range. This is my preferred placement for the stop-loss. It gives your position enough room to allow for dips, and, generally, if it heads back to break that former pullback low, it is a failed runner.

D) You can identify a large volume of bids on the Level 2 and put the stop below that. Be careful with this option; it should mainly be used as validation of support and as confirmation for one of the other options.

Here's a chart outlining the breakout entry:

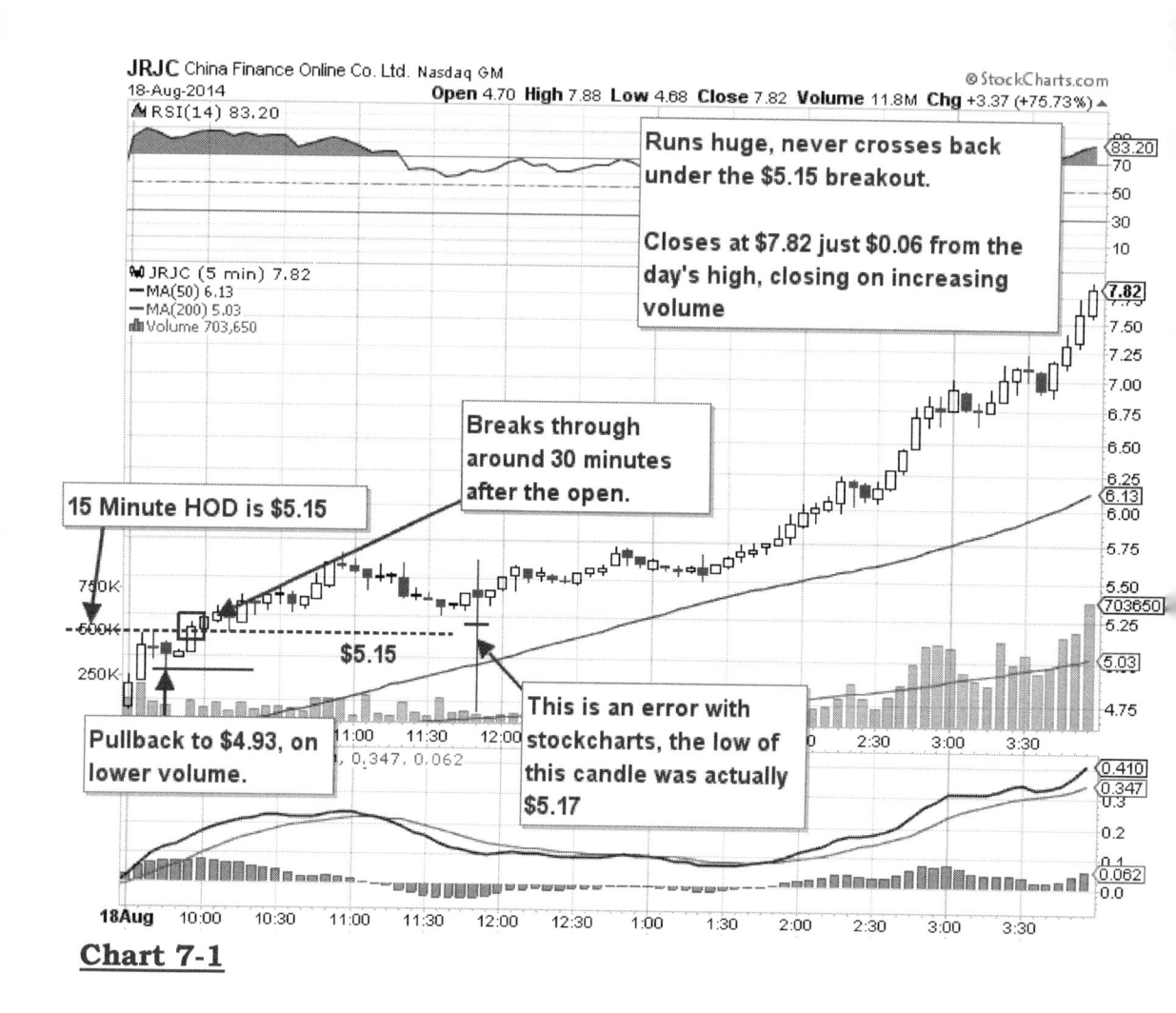

JRJC China Finance Online Co. Ltd. Nasdaq GM — 18-Aug-2014 — Open 4.70 High 7.88 Low 4.68 Close 7.82 Volume 11.8M Chg +3.37 (+75.73%)

Annotations on chart:
- Runs huge, never crosses back under the $5.15 breakout.
- Closes at $7.82 just $0.06 from the day's high, closing on increasing volume
- 15 Minute HOD is $5.15
- Breaks through around 30 minutes after the open.
- Pullback to $4.93, on lower volume.
- $5.15
- This is an error with stockcharts, the low of this candle was actually $5.17

Chart 7-1

So as we're watching this alerted stock, after it sets its fifteen-minute high of $5.15, we place our conditional order. For our stop-limit purchase order, the stop price is $5.16 ($0.01 above the high). Your buy limit would vary based on your preferences and individual circumstances, but let's say we set it with the stop at $5.16 and limit of $5.19.

The "stop-on-quote" sell order is placed at the same time. Your options for the stop price are:
    A) $4.92 ($0.01 below the pullback's low)

- Risk is $0.25-$0.27 per share

B) $4.99 ($0.01 below the $5.00 whole number)
- Risk is $0.18-$0.20 per share

C) $5.14 ($0.01 below the $5.15 former high)
- Risk is $0.03-$0.05 per share

Here is what the order looks like in E*Trade:

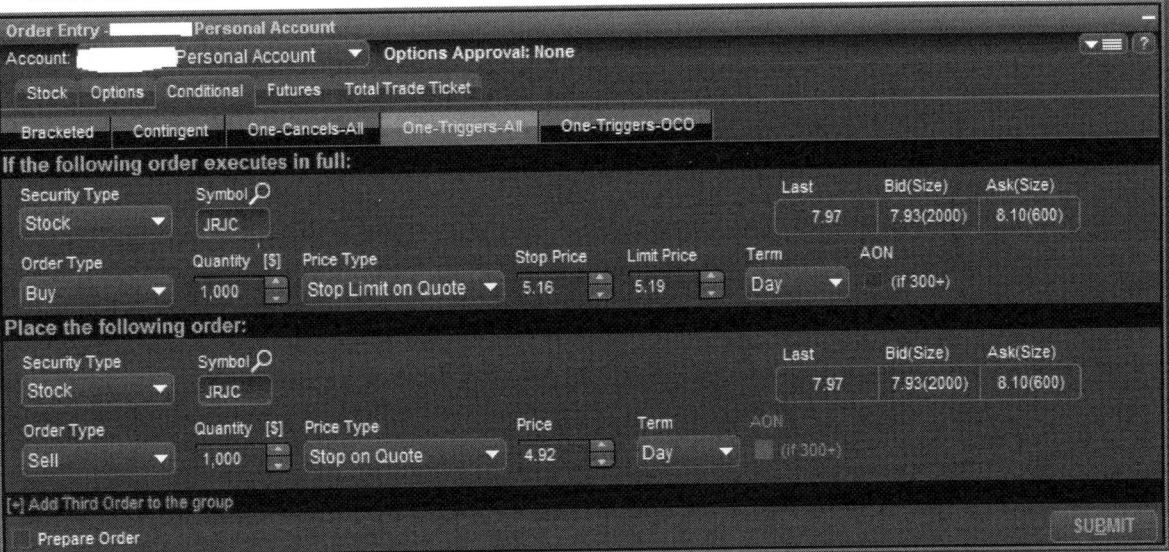

You can see in the graphic above, we chose a "Conditional" "One-Triggers-All" order, and then placed the stop-limit buy order and stop-on-quote sell order.

Let's go over the red flag/green flag review on this one just to see what it looked like:

Chart 7-2

After it breaks the $5.00 level, there isn't any more resistance until it gets up to the $6 level, and it goes on to blow right through that.

So now you know how to go about executing the breakout entry.

You need to understand that the most important component of your entry has nothing to do with your order. It occurs during your red/green review. A thoughtful analysis during your red flag/green flag review will keep you out of most low-reward setups.

You always want a minimum reward of 3x your risk. So if you estimate most stops will put you at a risk exposure between $0.10 and $0.30 per share, you want the setup you're reviewing to have enough room to run up appropriately for that amount of risk.

Keep in mind your entry will be above the fifteen-minute high. If you're looking at a stock that has just opened, during your review you need to make sure the resistance areas are significantly above the current price to allow for a minimum 3x reward.

When executing your entry on those setups with a positive green flag review, you will be in trades with a high probability of significant upward price movement at a price point that offers low risk, high reward.

The next step is the other half of the equation—closing the trade and taking profits.

Chapter 8 – Taking Profits

Your ability to exit a trade appropriately may be the most important factor in your success with this strategy. In order to be profitable long-term with these setups, you need to let the runners run.

After your entry, switch to a five-minute chart to monitor the progress and identify exits.

If after your entry you're unable to monitor your trade after the initial opening hour, you'll need to check in periodically using your brokerage's smartphone app to manage your trade/adjust your stop.

Trust me, not being in front of the computer watching the minute-to-minute price movement of your trade is often a good thing. At the end of this chapter, I give a few options for modified exits you can use if you're only able to check the trade periodically.

There are three components that will allow you to get the most out of your trade:

1) Identify resistance levels and adjust your stop appropriately.

2) Move your stop up following pullbacks and new HOD breakouts.

3) Trust what the volume and candles are telling you.

Let's touch on each . . .

Identify Resistance and Adjust Stop
You should have identified resistance during your red flag/green flag review on any setups you enter. Once the price gets up to the level of resistance, cancel your standing stop-loss order and replace it with either a stop-on-quote order immediately under the current price or use a trailing stop, if available, and pay very close attention to the candles/volume at resistance levels.

Move Your Stop Up Incrementally
Moving your stop up to break even, as soon as the situation allows, removes all risk from the trade. So you basically have a free ride toward profit once the price action allows for the stop to be moved up to this level. Don't do this too early, or you will be stopped out and potentially miss a major upward price move.

Additionally, moving your stop up incrementally following new highs and pullbacks, as well as moving them up when the price action/volume dictate, will lock you into guaranteed profits while allowing for further potential gains.

Generally, the opportunity to move your stop up to break even will present itself after a post-breakout pullback, when a dip occurs before the price moves up again.

Trust the Volume and Price Action
Always remain vigilant as to what the candles are indicating about what's going on "behind the scenes" and the associated volume. The majority of the time, you can count on the volume and price action to lead you to the correct decision. Volume and price action rarely lie; make sure you're constantly practicing and working on improving your skill in their analysis.

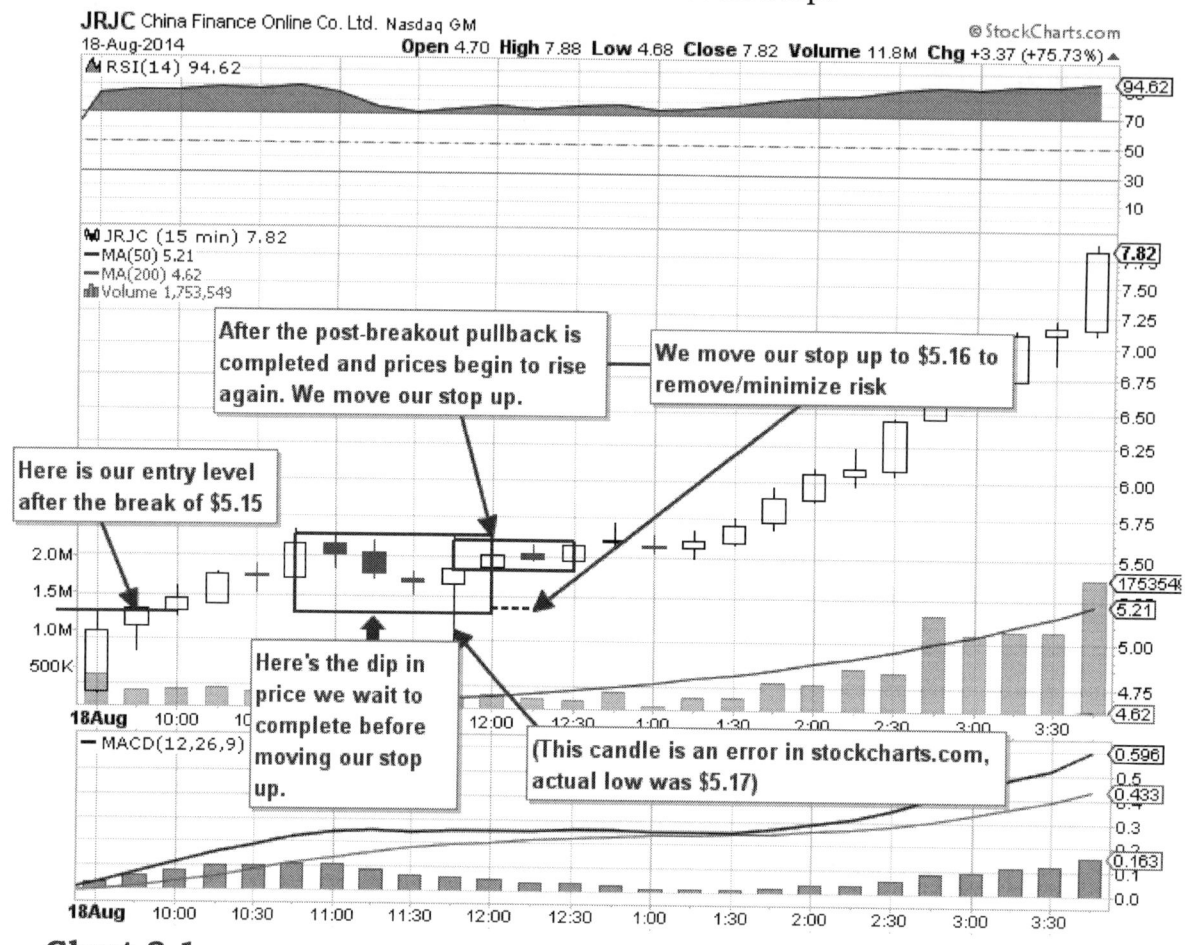

Here is an illustration of the initial break-even stop:

Chart 8-1

How the stop should advance subsequently:

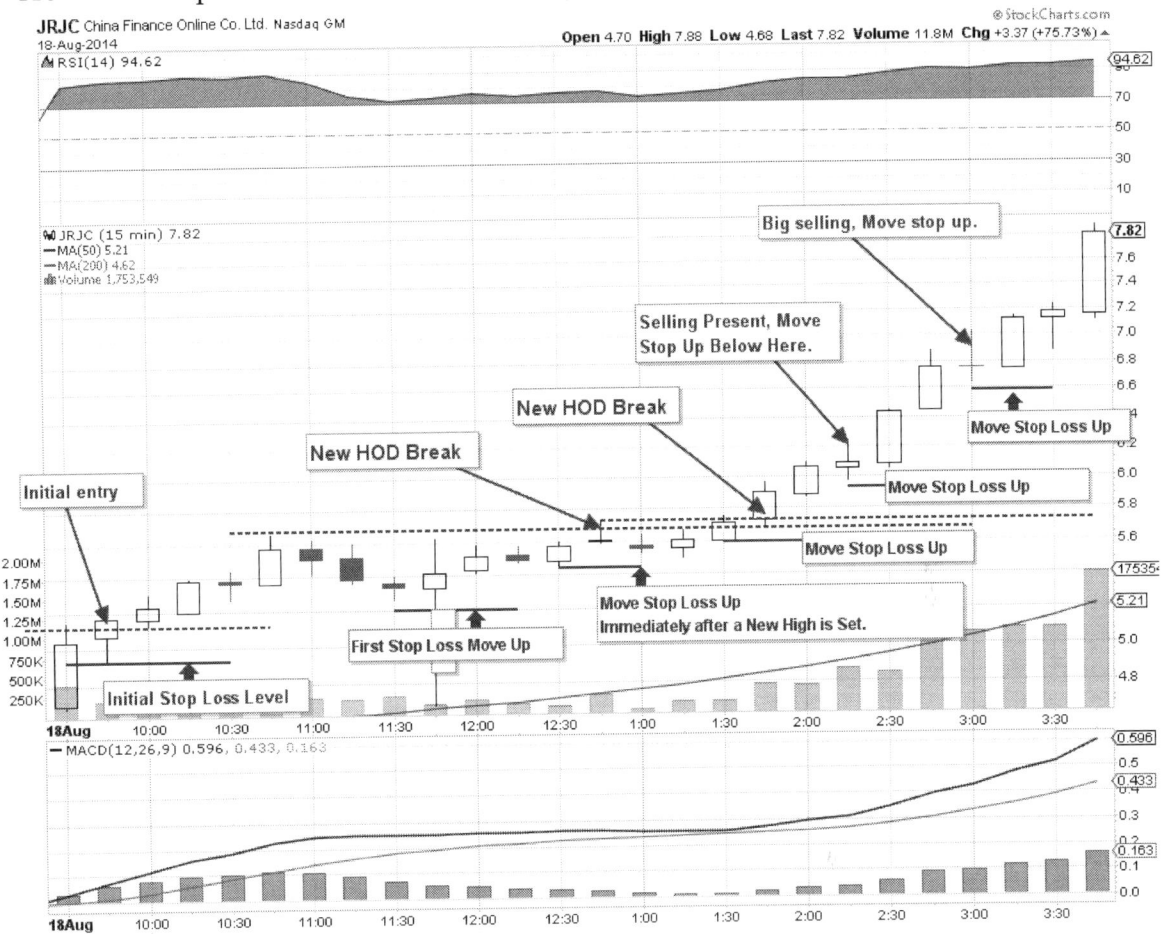

Chart 8-2

If you're only able to monitor the trade infrequently during the day, here is a modified practice for managing your stop-loss/profit protection sell order:

After your breakout entry is executed, you can cancel your current stop-loss order (which was triggered automatically with the entry order) and replace it with a "One-Cancels-All" order. A One-Cancels-All order is similar to a One-Triggers-All order, in which we place two trades at the same time; except any time one of the orders is executed, the other is cancelled.

So what we would do in our JRJC example is, after our entry, we would enter two separate sell orders. One would be the stop-on-quote sell order with our stop set at $4.92 (or another option of your choosing), which is the stop-loss order; the other would be a stop-limit order, with the stop at a level above the current price, which would sell you out of your position for a profit.

If you must use this practice because you're unable to monitor your trade during the day, make sure you put your upper, profit-taking sell order at a level just below where you see a resistance level. Don't be greedy; set it below resistance.

Keep in mind you're going to want it at a level at least 3x higher than your stop-loss level (For instance, in our example, our risk per trade is around $0.26 [$5.18 entry - $4.92 stop-loss], so we're looking for at least 3/1, which is $0.78 per share, or an exit of $5.96 [$5.18 entry + $0.78]).

If there is a resistance level below that 3x price, you shouldn't be in the trade in the first place. If resistance is significantly above that price, you may be able to move it higher and still be safe; you'll have to use your judgment.

But know this—the worst possible thing you can do is allow a successful trade with a nice profit to turn around and become a loss for you. If you are unable to monitor your trade and manage your stop-loss during the day, err on the side of conservative caution.

Obviously, the downside to this method is that your profit is limited to your upper sale price, even if the price continues much higher. I'm not sure if other brokerages allow it, but in E*Trade, you cannot enter a stop order that triggers a trailing stop, which would be useful here to guarantee a profit if executed while allowing the potential for further upward price movement.

I've been lobbying them to build this type of order capability into their system without much luck thus far. ☺

The next chapter is dedicated to reviewing several recent alerts, so you can build your awareness and begin to think about optimal stop-loss/profit management.

Chapter 9 – Chart Review

This chapter outlines real charts alerted for our setup the last 20 days or so of this writing. For each setup, I'll walk through the daily review on the first chart and the order decisions on a second five-minute chart.

I've put sample orders on the charts; this doesn't necessarily mean an order should have been placed. It's merely to outline what would have happened had an order been placed. Remember, if there aren't green flags present, or too many red flags appear, an order should not be placed.

Also, in several of the "sample orders," a stop-loss option is given at $0.01 below the breakout level. As I wrote earlier, this isn't really a viable option as it gets taken out too easily, but I've listed it as an option below to make you aware that it does get taken out regularly before the price runs up.

Chart 9-1

AMCF opens on a huge gap up, which is a red flag. It's extended pretty far above the 200 and 50-day simple moving averages as well, which doesn't help bring in heavy buying. It opens right above support at the $2.50 level, which would be good if the other red flags weren't present.

- 65 -

Chart 9-2

A trade never triggers; notice the first candle has a very long upper wick, indicating a lot of selling pressure.

Chart 9-3

APT opens with a very small gap and immediately above a significant support level at $2.30. Both are good signs, but we see there's a resistance level at $2.50.

- 67 -

Chart 9-4

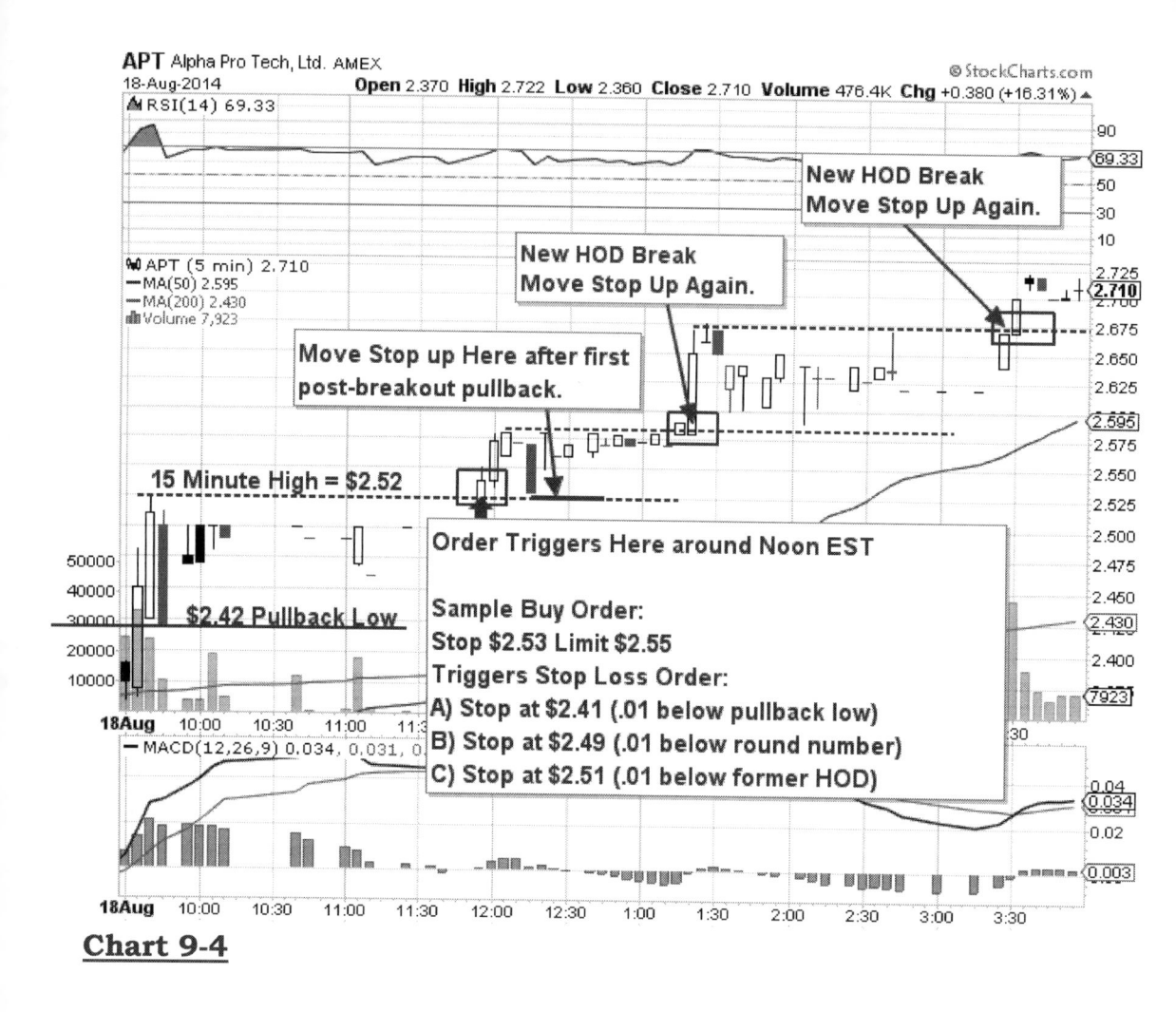

Recalling the $2.50 resistance area on the daily chart, the first fifteen-minute high is right at this level. Notice the fourth candle is selling off, but has significantly less volume than the prior three bullish candles. $2.49 would seem a good place for your stop-loss order after a breakout, but that is very close to the entry; so you may want to put it a little lower at $2.41.

After the order triggers, we are able to move up our stop to break-even shortly after the first post-breakout pullback. On each subsequent High of Day break we move our stop up again, locking in profits. Our stops never being taken out, we would sell prior to the close around $2.70-$2.71, and would realize a gain of $0.17-$0.20 per share. APT closes the day at $2.71, up about 15% on the day.

Chart 9-5

ARO opens on a 13% gap up. Its open is immediately above $3.50 support, which is good. It broke above its 50-day SMA, which is good. $4.00 resistance is the next level where we can expect selling pressure; we should probably take profits if it gets up to that level.

Chart 9-6

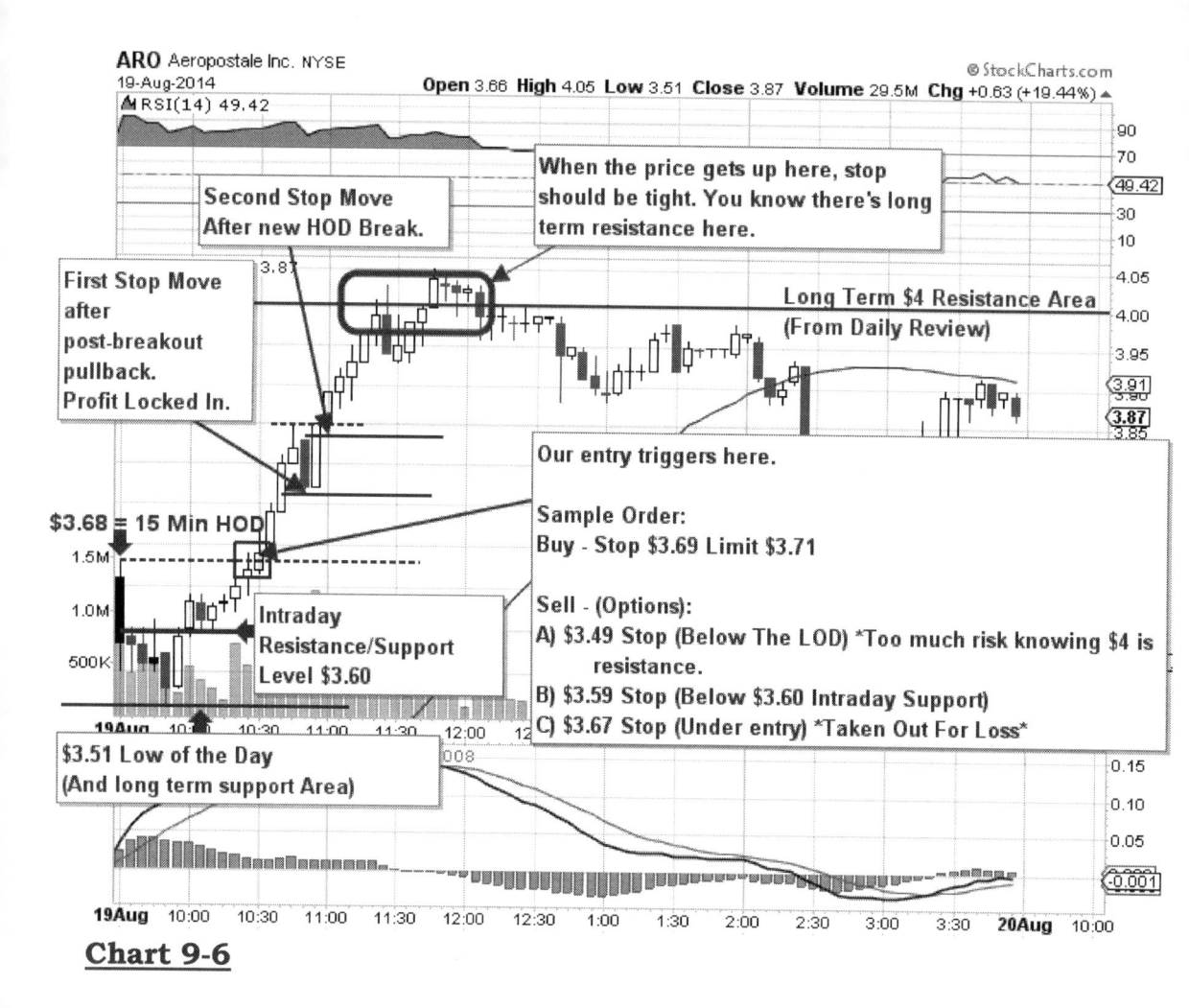

It breaks the fifteen-minute high of $3.68, triggering an order, and doesn't dip back under it. We move our stop up after pullbacks and new HOD breaks, removing risk and then locking in profits. As expected right around the $4 level, selling comes in and prevents it from running higher. We either exit or get stopped out in the $3.90-$4 range with a profit of $0.20-$0.30 per share.

Chart 9-7

BSPM opens with very little gap up. This is a good sign. It has $1.25 support below, but it's looking at a 50-day SMA of $1.38 immediately above its open price, as well as $1.50 resistance. If it can get through that, $1.80 resistance and $1.81 200-day SMA.

Chart 9-8

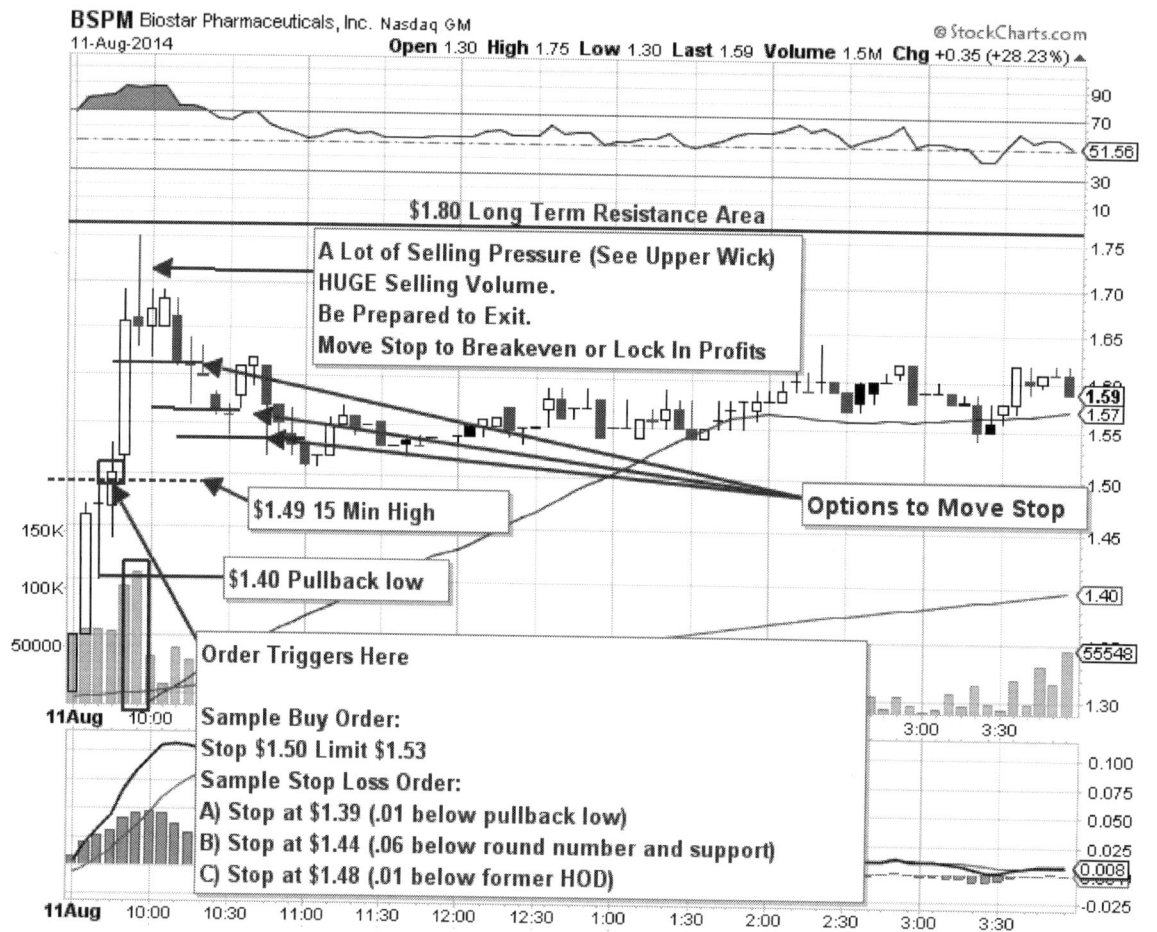

We know there's resistance at $1.50, and this is right about where the fifteen-minute opening range high is set ($1.49). If it breaks this resistance, our order will trigger.

We know to expect major selling resistance at the $1.80 level, so it wouldn't be unwise to take profits or place an extremely tight stop after it started approaching that area (like after it starts making new highs in the $1.70s).

After seeing the huge volume and selling pressure at the red candle with the long upper wick, if we haven't taken profits yet, we need to get ready

- 72 -

to exit and move the stop at least to the point where we would break even. This trade would most likely have resulted in a marginal gain or break-even.

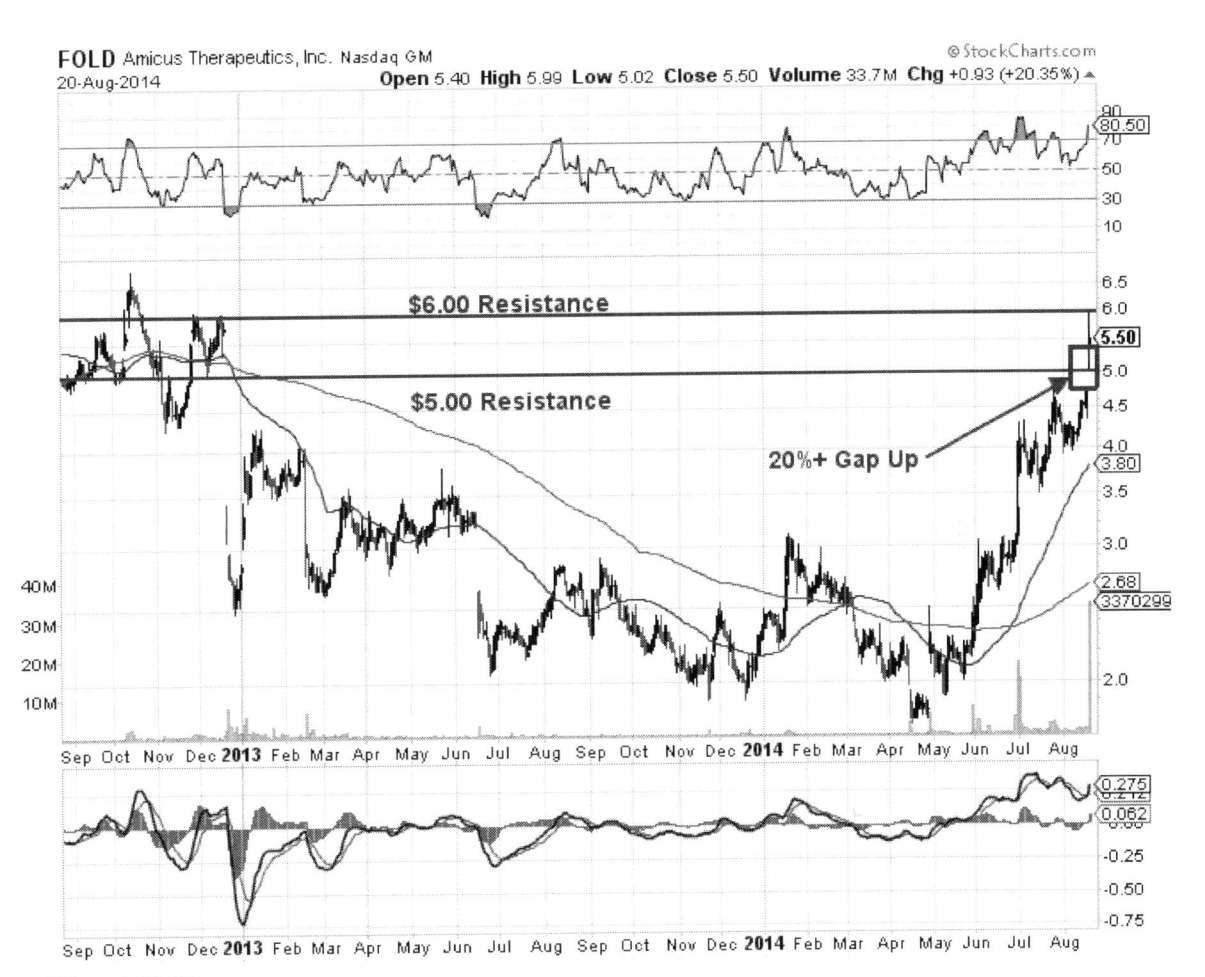

Chart 9-9

FOLD opens with huge relative volume above $5.00 support, and we see we're likely to run into selling at the $6 level. In addition to what we see detailed on the chart, you should be aware when doing your review that this price is pretty far extended above and away from both its 200-day and 50-day SMA, not green flags.

- 73 -

Chart 9-10

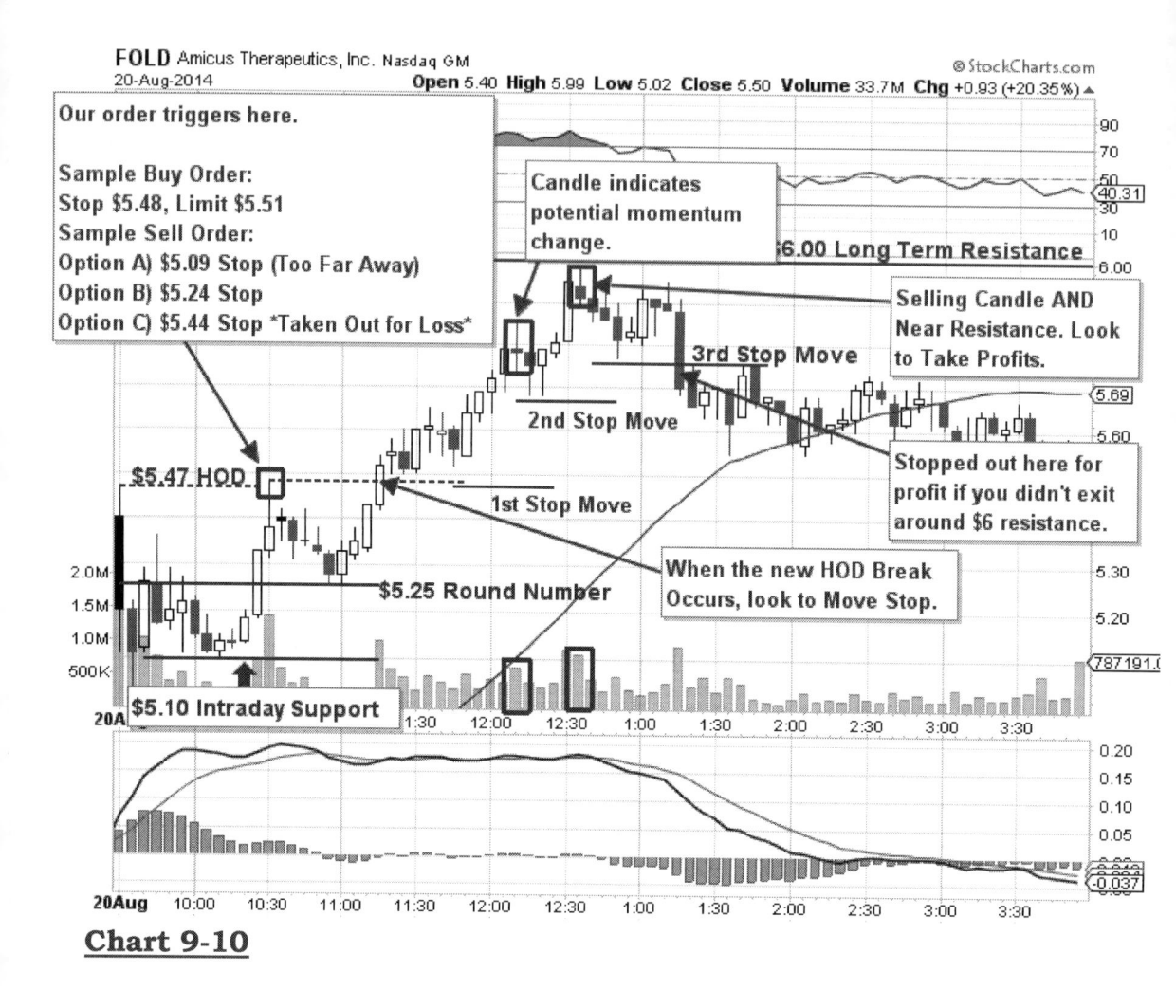

This setup is actually much better suited to a low entry rather than a breakout entry, but again, that's for another book.

If we had placed an entry order on this setup, we'd have been taken out for a loss, unless we had our stop at $5.24, right below that round $5.25 number. As usual, when new HODs are broken, we move our stop up to minimize or remove risk and then to lock in profits.

Expectedly, the $6 resistance is the high of the day; the smart move would be to sell and take the profits right by that $6 level or move to a very tight stop around that level.

- 74 -

Chart 9-11

GV opens immediately above a major support level, around $1.67 and the 50-day SMA, both green flags. Notice the long-term resistance levels and 200-day SMA above, starting around $1.90. Depending on what price the fifteen-minute high is, this could be a good setup or not.

- 75 -

Chart 9-12

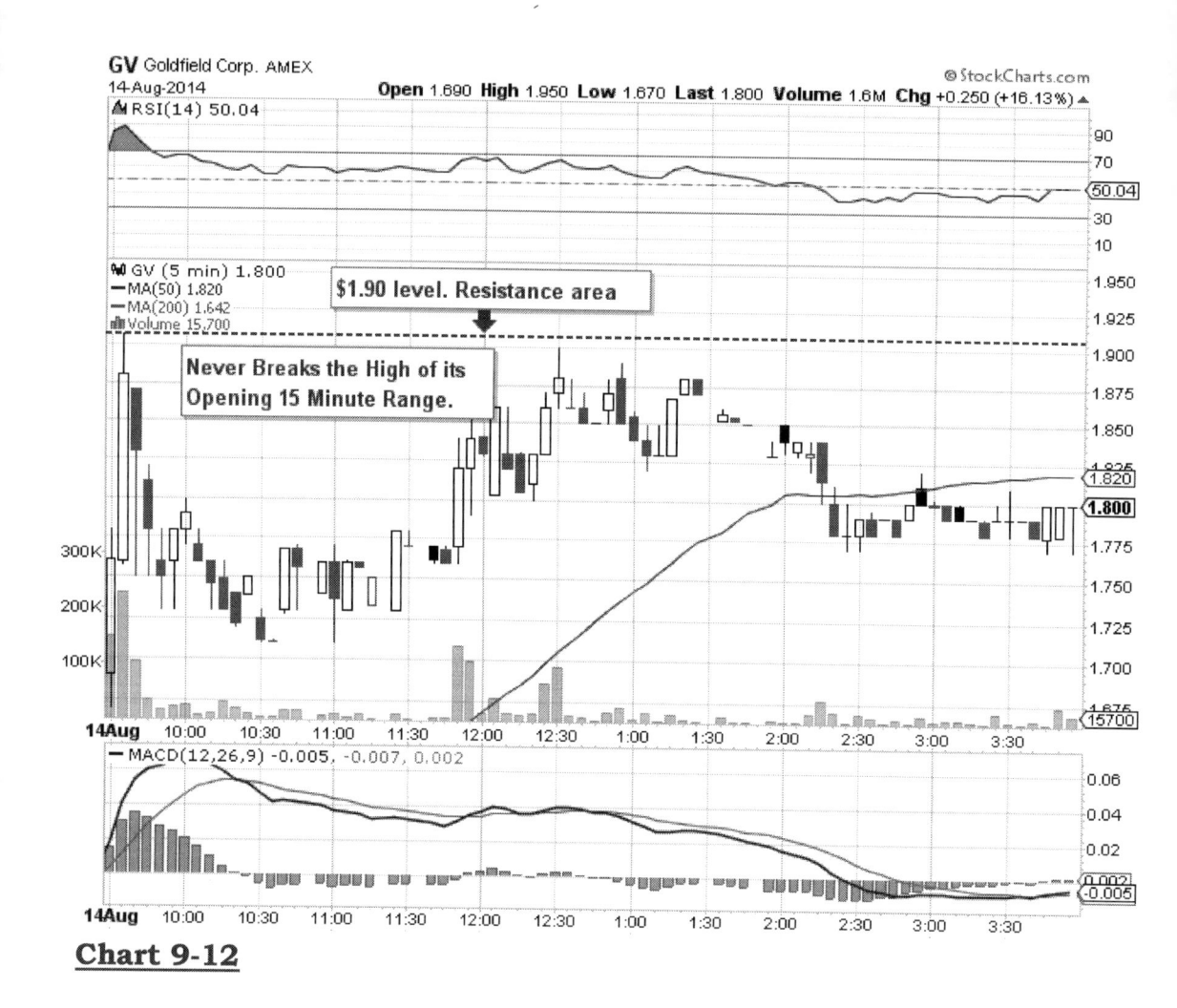

It runs up from $1.67 to the $1.90 resistance in the first ten minutes, so our breakout entry level is already at major resistance. It never breaks; no trade is triggered. No trade should have been placed.

As we can see on the daily chart, we could expect more resistance at the $2.10 level, even if it broke $1.90 resistance; so that doesn't leave us with much room for reward.

Chart 9-13

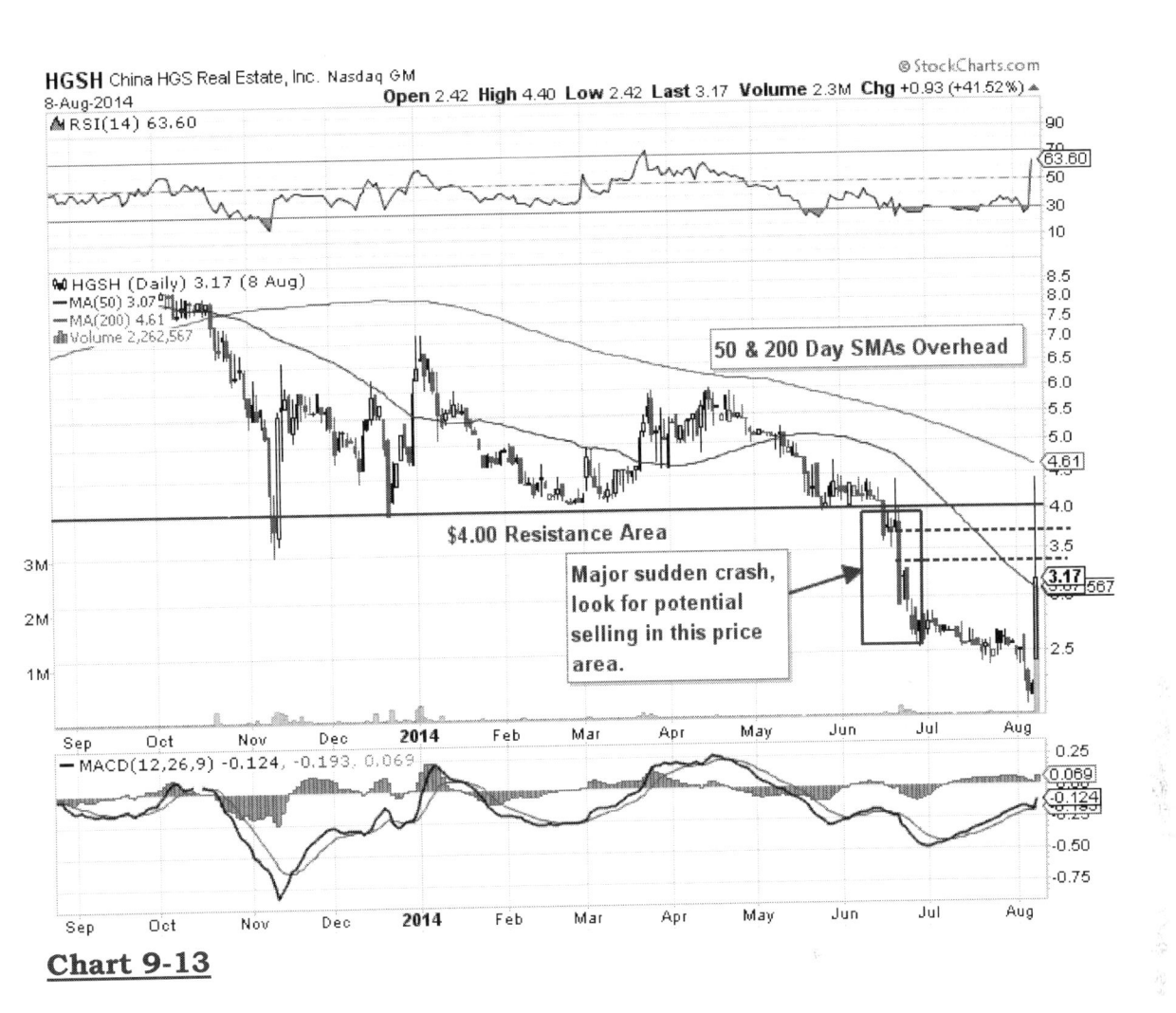

HGSH opens around $2.50 with a major price drop—red flag recently; it's got a serious $4.00 resistance level, and the 50-day SMA overhead at $3.17. These are all red flags.

Chart 9-14

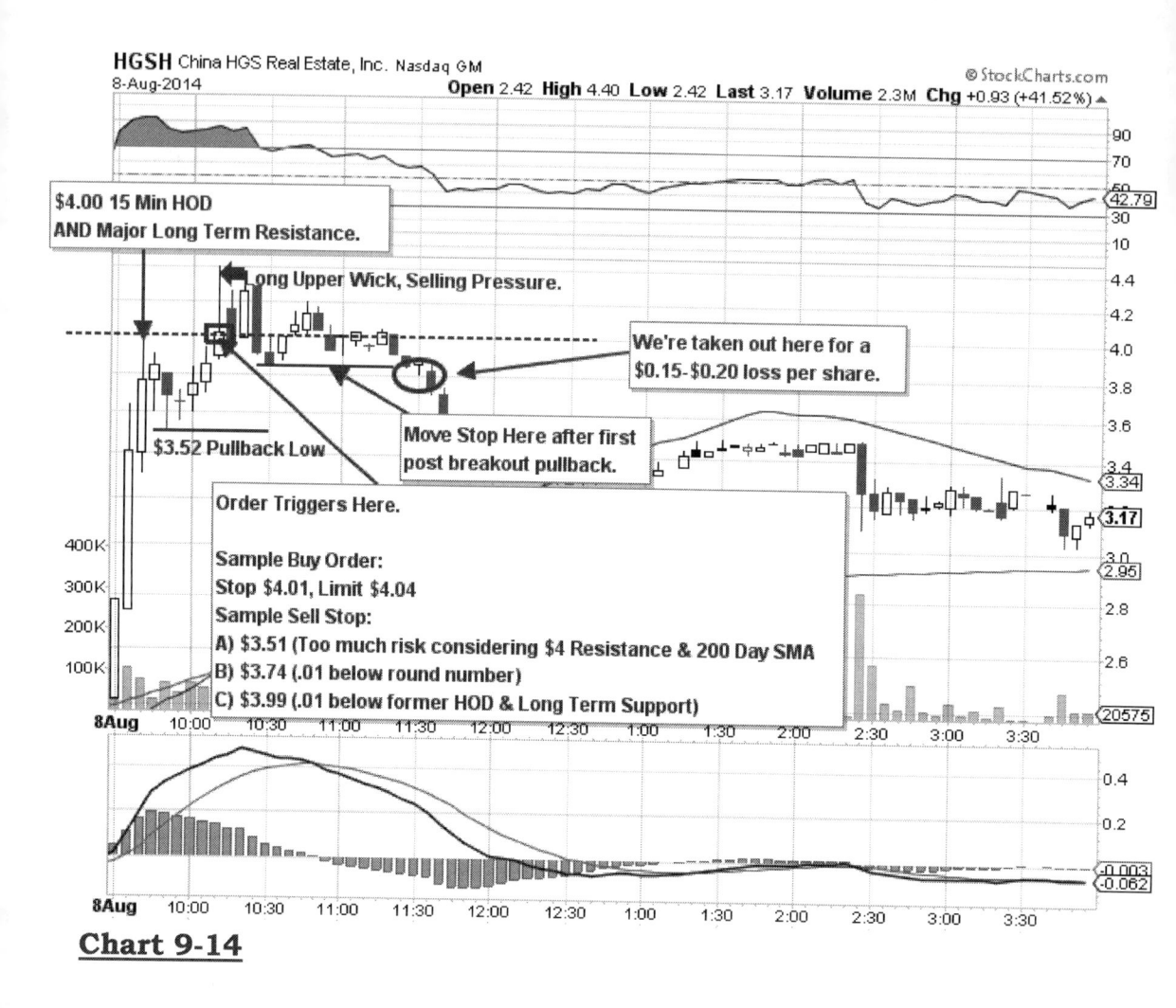

The fifteen-minute high of the day is $4.00, already at major resistance. We shouldn't be in this trade. If you were to gamble on it, you should maintain a very tight stop and be very vigilant about taking profits.

Chart 9-15

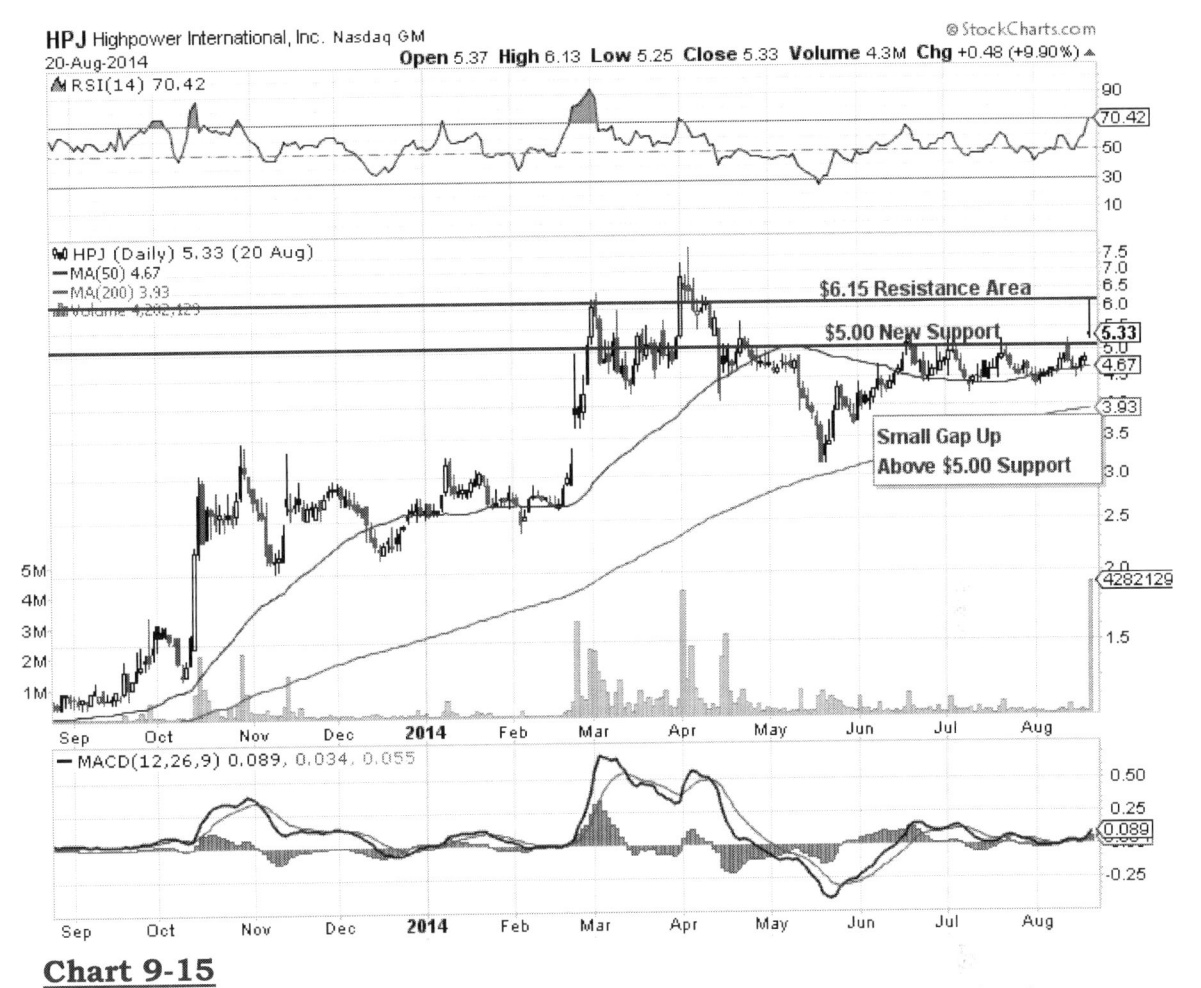

HPJ opens above $5 support, with a small gap up, looking at $6-$6.15 resistance area overhead.

Chart 9-16

While the trade never triggers, the $5.99 stop would be your best bet. Knowing there's the long-term resistance area around $6.15, look to move up to break even quickly.

Chart 9-17

HTBX opens at $5.15, around 25% higher than the previous day's close, which is a big red flag. It's got support at $5, which is good. $6 resistance is overhead, as well as the 200-day simple moving average at $6.27, and beyond that $7 resistance.

Here's the five-Minute:

(Chart showing HTBX Heat Biologics, Inc. Nasdaq CM, 21-Aug-2014, Open 5.15 High 6.84 Low 5.14 Close 5.30 Volume 1.4M Chg +1.16 (+28.02%))

Annotations on chart:
- $6.37 15Min HOD
- After we see this candle moving up we potentially move our stop to that initial pullback low. We'd get stopped out for a loss soon after.
- $6 Support
- Order Triggers Here
- Sample Buy Order: Stop $6.37, Limit $6.40
- Sample Sell Order:
  A) $5.99 Stop (.01 below round number and support)
  B) $6.24 Stop (.01 below round number)

Chart 9-18

It has a major move of more than 20% in the first ten minutes of the opening range. This was a tough one for a breakout entry and another that's better suited to a low entry.

The breakout entry level is $6.37, which doesn't offer a significant reward, knowing that $7 resistance is lurking above waiting to crush buying momentum.

There isn't a whole lot we can do to avoid taking a loss on something that acts like this, other than staying out or maintaining vigilance to take profits quickly when it approaches $7.

Chart 9-19

INPH is very similar to the HGSH setup we already reviewed; it opens on high relative volume with significant $3.50 resistance overhead and a major price crash recently.

Chart 9-20
No trade is triggered; all the gains are during the opening range.

Chart 9-21

LRAD opens with a 12% gap up and has major support at the $1.94-$2.10 area, due to price support levels, as well as both the 50 and 200-day SMAs. There is $2.20 resistance it will have to contend with for any significant gains.

Chart 9-22

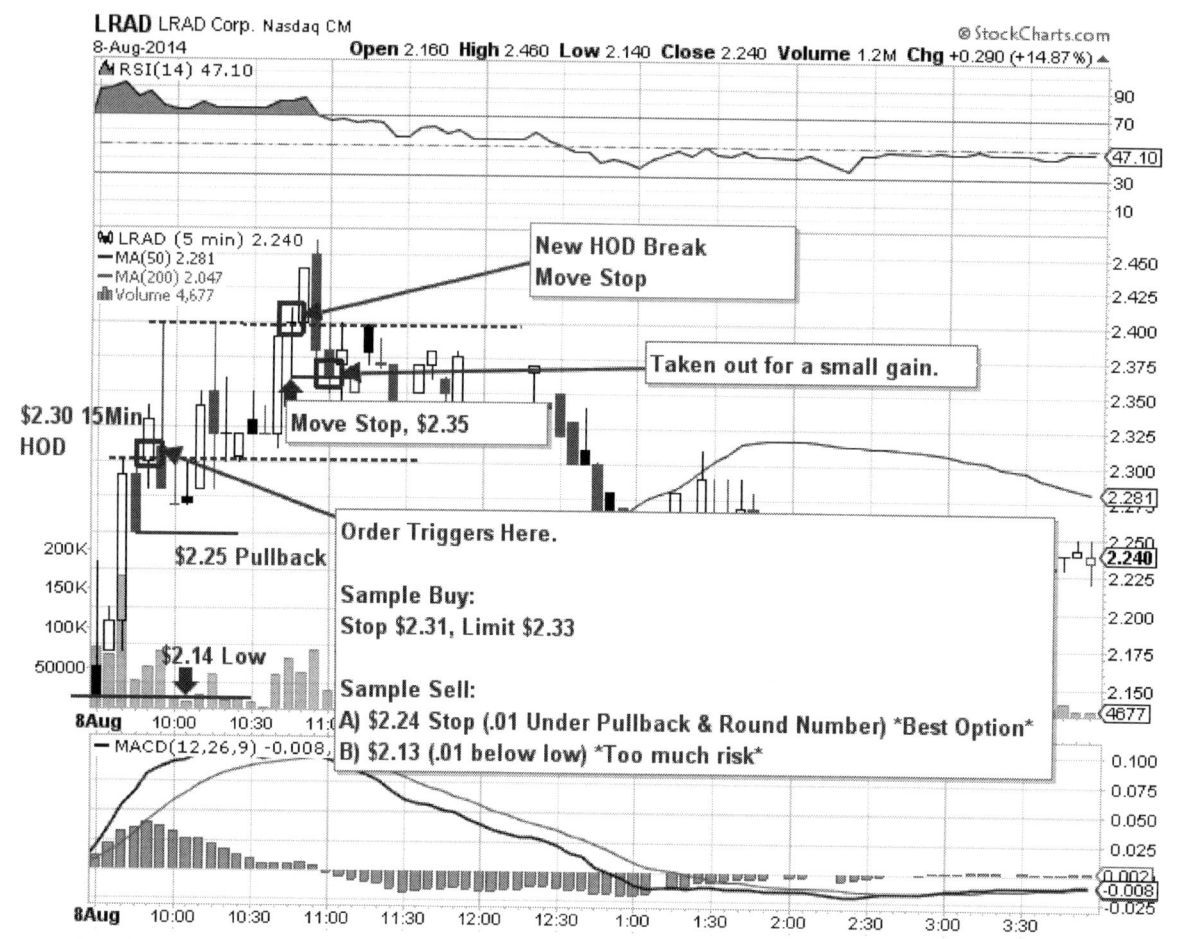

The opening fifteen-minute range sees $2.20 resistance broken and a pullback to $2.25. Our entry triggers on a break of $2.30. As we move our stop up after new HOD breaks, this trade ends up with a small gain.

Chart 9-23

SSH opens at $4.78 on an 8% gap up, which is not too large. It's got $5.40 resistance overhead as well as the $5.22 level at the 50-day simple moving average.

Chart 9-24

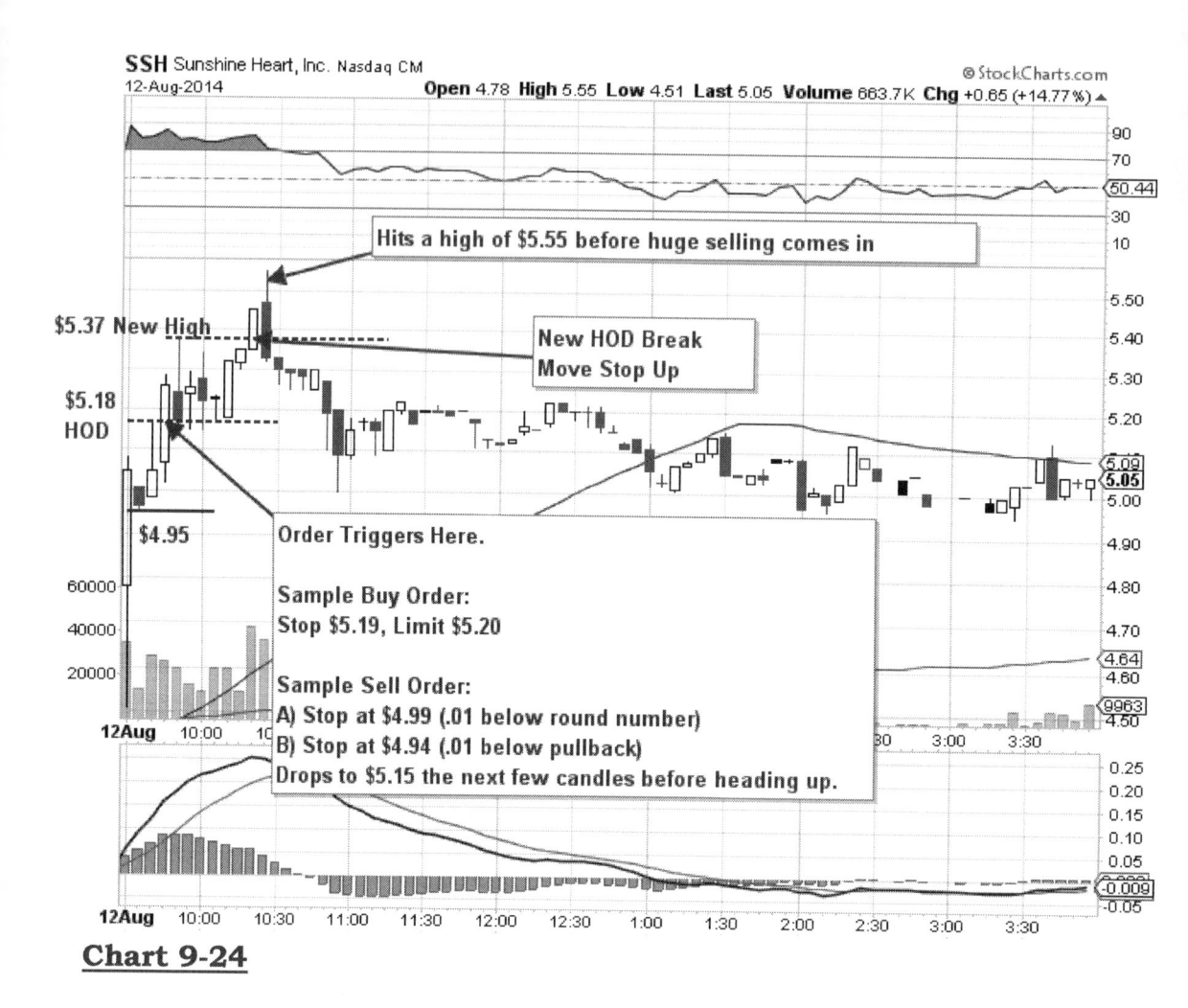

You'd know the price would run into heavy selling getting into the $5.40 area and above. When there's a break of the $5.37 new high, we should move our stop up to lock in profits and keep the stop tight because we're in major resistance territory.

Hopefully, these charts and review notes help prepare you for real-time analysis of these setups. I will tell you that, while it's easy to look back on a chart and identify what you should have done, it becomes very difficult when watching a five-minute chart in real-time. The chart doesn't appear as it does above; the individual bars fill the chart screen, and it takes practice to identify unfolding patterns.

To identify the ideal places for entries, stops, etc., you need to

A) maintain patience and discipline,

B) analyze the volume and candles as they unfold, and

C) trust what your price action/volume analysis is telling you.

Most importantly, you need to be diligent and thoughtful in your red/green flag review. This will put you into successful setups, warn you of levels where you need to be looking to take profits, and keep you out of those setups that have a higher chance of failing.

Chapter 10 – Step-By-Step Recap

We're nearly done, this chapter serves as an overview of the strategy.

Step One – Identifying Potential High Volume Runners:
(Chapter 5)

We are scanning for NYSE, Nasdaq, and AMEX stocks priced between $1 and $10, with volume at least 30 times higher than average for the time of day, trading at 30,000 volume minimum, and priced at least 4% higher than the closing price of the prior day. We also have a secondary, redundant scan looking for stocks up a minimum of 6% for the day, with the same price range and minimum volume.

As the stocks are alerted we first verify that they are liquid enough to trade.

Step Two – Qualifying the Setup:
(Chapter 6)

Red Flag Review:

1) Is there a significant price resistance level(s) overhead based on the weekly and/or daily chart?

2) Are there any abrupt price crashes in the nearby past which could mean former buyers holding through those crashes will look to sell for a chance to break-even?

3) Is the gap up from the prior day large enough that current holders will be scrambling to sell to take profits?

- 90 -

4) Where are the medium to long term Simple Moving Average lines? If they are above the current price, they may serve as areas of strong selling.

Green Flag Review:

1) Is there a significant level of buying support immediately below the current price level based on the weekly and/or daily chart?

2) Is the price action over the last 3 to 12 months in a tight range with light volume?

3) Is the current price at or about to be at a new long-term high?

4) Is the current price breaking above long to medium term simple moving averages?

Step Three – Entering the Order:
(Chapter 7)

After qualifying a potential setup we determine our trade size either by a mental calculation or using the 'trade size' excel tool. We then prepare a One-Triggers-All entry order.

The Buy order we enter is a 'Stop-Limit' order, with the stop price set at $0.01 higher than the highest price of the first 15 Minutes, and the Limit purchase price set at a few cents higher than the stop price.

The Sell order (our Stop-loss / loss limit order) portion of the One-Triggers-All entry is set as a "Stop on Quote" order. The Stop price is set, using your discretion, somewhere just below a round number and/or the pullback low of the opening range. If hit, the order becomes a market sell order to exit the trade for a small loss.

Step Four – Managing the Order & Taking Profits:
(Chapter 8)

You've identified levels of potential resistance during your red/green qualifying review of the setup. Your immediate concern, if your entry order has executed, is to determine if the price is quickly rising into this level of likely resistance; if so, take profits at this level or move your stop up just under this level to protect your profits and remove the risk of loss.

Monitor the trade using a 5 minute chart. As new Highs are set and pullbacks occur, incrementally move your stop loss order up below these new highs and pullbacks to remove risk and lock in profits. Always be vigilant of the resistance levels you've identified and act accordingly.

Analyze the volume/price action combination and trust what the volume and candles are revealing to you about the likely movement of the price.

Step Five – Post Trade Analysis:
Keep a trade journal of every trade you enter, and run "post-game analysis", like you're watching game tapes. Consistently analyzing your trade performance is the best way to improve.

You should take a screen shot of the weekly & daily chart for your trade, and a screen shot of a full day's 5 minute chart for your trade. Note your entry price, your original stop level, any subsequent moves in the stop, and your exit price.

Look at the daily and weekly chart, how did your red/green flag review hold up? Did you miss anything? What'd you get right?

Dig in to the day's activity and note any significant moments of volume/price action. Compare the activity to your original red/green review. What did you do well? Where is there room for improvement? Where were you correct in your volume/price action analysis? Where were you incorrect? Did you capture a large range of the movement? Why or why not?

Sometimes a stock's price movement will shake us out of the trade and leave us missing a large movement. At times it'll happen and it's unavoidable, other times it happens because we read the price action wrong, or we didn't locate appropriate resistance levels, etc.

Keep a detailed trade journal and focus on continuous improvement. Analyze and improve, repeat.

Final Remarks & Contact Info

So there it is—just about everything I have to give you on this particular strategy without letting the book get too bogged down. Since this is the first revision, my plan is to take the questions and comments I get from readers and add updated revisions as well as perhaps videos and blogs to cover those questions.

In order to receive updates to this book, please sign up for the free blog at www.langhamtrading.com, or email your order form for this book to Orders@1HourTrade.com for a free month of platinum level membership and access to our live trading room and analysis material.

I sincerely hope I've given you the value you wanted and expected in this book and equipped you with the tools you need to capitalize on this setup. I tried to create a book that I would have liked to have when starting out, and I believe I've accomplished that. If you bought this book and you disagree, email me; we'll work it out. I don't want to leave any of my readers feeling they've not received a fair exchange.

If you liked this book, I would be very much in your debt and supremely grateful if you will **please take one minute and provide a review for it here:** http://www.amazon.com/dp/B00OAW29EE

If you hated this book, I would be very much in your debt and supremely grateful if you would stay away from this book's review section ☺

Please feel free to email me any time with questions, comments, concerns, criticism, or anything else you'd like, at brian@1hourtrade.com; I will reply.

And please join our Facebook community/discussion group for readers:
https://www.facebook.com/groups/1HourTrade/
We discuss variations on strategy, reader questions, at times there is commentary on my lack of a grasp of elementary grammar, etc.

Please take a moment to **Follow me on Twitter**:
https://twitter.com/LanghamTrading
and **Like the Langham Facebook Page**:
https://www.facebook.com/langhamgroup

In the near future, I'll be putting out a few more books covering additional strategies that have proven successful, and I'll be building out the www.langhamtrading.com site as a trader community, information source, and educational platform. I hope you'll consider becoming a member; making money as a group is just more fun than doing it alone, and our trading chat room is a great place to get access to real-time analysis of these high volume runner setups as well as a number of other strategies.

Thank you very much for reading this book, truly. I wish you much success, and I hope this is merely the start of the connection we now share.

Made in the USA
Charleston, SC
24 July 2015